ḤESED IN THE BIBLE

THIS VOLUME IS GRATEFULLY DEDICATED
TO MRS. B. JOSEPH HAMMOND OF LOS ANGELES
WHOSE APPRECIATION FOR JEWISH SCHOLARSHIP
MADE THE PUBLICATION OF THIS WORK POSSIBLE

ḤESED IN THE BIBLE

by

NELSON GLUECK

Translated by

ALFRED GOTTSCHALK

With an introduction by

GERALD A. LARUE

Edited by

ELIAS L. EPSTEIN

WIPF & STOCK · Eugene, Oregon

Wipf and Stock Publishers
199 W 8th Ave, Suite 3
Eugene, OR 97401

Hesed in the Bible
By Glueck, Nelson and Gottschalk, Alfred

ISBN 13: 978-1-61097-124-9
Publication date 5/1/2011
Previously published by Hebrew Union College Press, 1967

Table of Contents

List of Abbreviations

A.S. — *Die Schriften des Alten Testaments in Auswahl übersetzt und für die Gegenwart erklärt.*

AJSL. — *American Journal of Semitic Languages and Literature.*

B.C. — *Biblischer Commentar über das Alte Testament,* ed. by C. F. Keil and F. Delitzsch.

B.H. — Kittel, R. *Biblia Hebraica.*

E.H. — *Kurzgefasstes exegetisches Handbuch zum Alten Testament.*

H.C. — *Kurzer Hand-Commentar zum Alten Testament,* ed. by K. Marti.

H.K. — *Handkommentar zum Alten Testament,* ed. by W. Nowack.

I.C.C. — *International Critical Commentary.*

K. — *Kommentar zum Alten Testament,* ed. by E. Sellin.

K.K. — *Kurzgefasster Kommentar zum Alten Testament,* ed. by H. Strack and O. Zöckler.

S.B.O.T. — *Sacred Books of the Old Testament,* ed. by P. Haupt.

ZAW. — *Zeitschrift für die alttestamentliche Wissenschaft.*

List of Abbreviations

Translator's Preface

Professor Nelson Glueck's pioneer study of *ḥesed* and its meaning in the Bible has long been a basic source for biblical scholarship and theology. When the work first appeared as a published doctoral dissertation in July 1927, titled *Das Wort ḥesed im alttestamentlichen Sprachgebrauche als menschliche und göttliche gemeinschaftsgemässe Verhaltungsweise*, it was a methodological landmark in the study of the history of ideas of the Bible. The work, republished in Germany in 1961, indicated that its findings were still valuable for contemporary research in biblical thought; therefore, an English translation was deemed appropriate in order to make it available to a wider circle of readers. Translations of biblical texts are from the German to keep the author's innovations and shadings of meaning.

To bring the discussion up to date, Dr. Gerald A. Larue, Professor of Biblical History and Archaeology, University of Southern California, consented to preface the translation with a summary of recent trends in studies on *ḥesed*.

I remain indebted in the preparation of my translation to Mrs. Helen Lederer of Cincinnati, who made an earlier attempt to render the work into English; to my colleagues, Dr. Hans Hirschberg of Tarzana, and Dr. Michael A. Meyer of the Hebrew Union College, for their valuable suggestions; to Mrs. Fae Cohen, secretary to the faculty of the Hebrew Union College, Los Angeles school, for her careful and painstaking assistance in the typing and preparation of the manuscript. However, final responsibility for editing and translating, as well as for any errors which may still remain, is my own.

Finally, I wish to note my deep gratitude to Professor Glueck for entrusting me with his work and for the many *ḥasadim* he has shown me.

ALFRED GOTTSCHALK
Hebrew Union College
Los Angeles, California

Recent Studies in *Ḥesed*

by

GERALD A. LARUE

The importance of Nelson Glueck's monograph on *ḥesed* is, perhaps, best demonstrated in the use made of his research in almost every important study involving the term since 1927, and in the relatively limited contributions made to Glueck's interpretation of the word. When *Lexicon in Veteris Testamenti Libros*, edited by Ludwig Köhler and Walter Baumgartner, appeared in 1951, the *ḥesed* reference not only utilized Glueck's work, but, in accordance with the editorial practise of noting definitive sources, listed Glueck's study as the authoritative work in the field.[1]

It is the purpose of this essay to recognize in chronological sequence significant studies of *ḥesed* made since the publication of Glueck's monograph, noting contributions made to the understanding of *ḥesed*. The intention is not to produce an exhaustive work, but to provide a broad but basic sampling, for, in addition to the works discussed below, countless other writings have utilized and built upon Glueck's research, generally acknowledging dependence in footnotes. Some scholars have compared or contrasted *ḥesed* with related terms. Some have sought to develop approaches to the study of the word that have led to different emphases in interpreting *ḥesed*. Some have simply duplicated the work done by Glueck. That still further study is called for should be clear from this report.

In the first article to build upon Glueck's study, W. F. Lofthouse compared *ḥen* and *ḥesed*.[2] He pointed out that in the verbal form *ḥen* referred to gracious and favorable action passing from a superior to an inferior — an action that could not be forced or demanded. The noun, which never appears in the plural form or without the definite article, is without religious significance and is rarely used of

[1] L. Köhler and W. Baumgartner, *Lexicon in Veteris Testamenti Libros* (Leiden: E. J. Brill, 1951), I, 318.

[2] W. F. Lofthouse, "*Ḥen* and *Ḥesed* in the Old Testament," *Zeitschrift für die Alttestamentliche Wissenschaft*, Vol. 51 (1933), pp. 29–35.

God, but is used of men between whom there neither is, nor can be, a specific bond. *Ḥen*, used in making a request, has the force of "please." In contrast, as Glueck has shown, *ḥesed* is employed only where a previous bond exists as in relationships of kinship, marriage, betrothal, guest-friendship, or alliance. *Ḥesed* is, therefore, opposite to *ḥen*. God's *ḥesed*, found in the covenant relationship, is rich and impressive and can be broken only by a man who has everything to lose, although God is also a loser. God's relationship to any breach of covenant is *ḥesed* which knows no alteration, and to which the defaulter may appeal.

In 1938 the Graduate School of Yale University accepted a dissertation by Boone A. Bowen, entitled *A Study of Ḥesed*.[3] Although Bowen is in basic agreement with Glueck that human *ḥesed* is, essentially, a beneficent expression of relationship growing out of some tie or bond such as a family or covenant or host-guest pattern, he develops other aspects of the term.

Methodologically, Bowen employs literary analysis of the text and establishes a rough historical development, enabling him to note unique usages produced by different writers, and particular emphases related to specific periods. His presentation is divided into seven general areas, representing *ḥesed* in the Hexateuch, early historical books, prophetic writings, wisdom literature, late historical books, the Megilloth and Daniel, and in the Psalms. J, E, D, P sources in the Hexateuch, Saul and Samuel sources in the historical books, "authentic" oracles and later additions in the prophetic writings, are recognized.

In J *ḥesed* is used twice to express human relationships (Gen. 24:49; 47:29). Divine *ḥesed*, manifesting in J Yahweh's fidelity to the covenantal bond, appears after the Abrahamic covenant is established (Gen. 15:18), and is related solely to persons embraced by the covenantal agreement.[4] There is no allusion to the *ḥesed* of *ʾelohim* in E, and only when the name "Yahweh" has been introduced in Exod. 3:14 ff. and the deity revealed as a covenantal God to Moses is the divine *ḥesed* mentioned (Exod. 15:13). As a human quality *ḥesed* represents reciprocal kindness or "loyal kindness."[5] The Deuteronomists never use *ḥesed* as a human quality, and when the term is used in reference to God it is always in close relationship to *bᵉrit*. The nation is the recipient of the divine *ḥesed* and the conditions under

[3] Boone A. Bowen, "A Study of חסד" (Unpublished dissertation, Yale University, 1938).

[4] *Ibid.*, p. 39. [5] *Ibid.*, p. 45.

which Israel can obtain the benefits of this *ḥesed* are stipulated. Both Israel and Yahweh have covenantal responsibilities and unless Israel obeys and loves Yahweh the nation cannot expect to receive the divine *ḥesed*. The responsibility of God to show *ḥesed* is, therefore, conditional in Deuteronomy, Bowen believes. The term *ḥesed* does not appear in the Priestly writings. Once again Bowen suggests that the phrase "loyal kindness" is an acceptable translation of *ḥesed*.

In the historical writings Bowen recognizes a Samuel (Sm) and a Saul (Sl) source. In Sl the two references to divine *ḥesed* (II Sam. 2:6; 15:20) concern Yahweh's loyalty to the king and Yahweh's appreciation of those showing devotion or rendering service to the anointed ruler. In II Sam. 15:20 Yahweh shows *ḥesed* to Ittai the Gittite who is, according to Bowen, "practically a stranger to the king," and Bowen finds it is unusual for Yahweh to show *ḥesed* to a foreigner. As a social quality *ḥesed* appears in eight passages, five referring to loyalty to the king and the royal family (II Sam. 2:5; 3:8; 10:2; 16:17; I Kings 2:7), and three pertaining to obligations of a covenantal promise (II Sam. 9:1, 3, 7). In Sm *ḥesed* is never found as a divine attribute and only once in I Sam. 15:6 as a social quality, and here, Bowen argues, the basis of *ḥesed* rests in a common religious affiliation, belief in the same God, not, as Glueck has suggested, in the marriage of Moses to a Kenite woman. He suggests that Glueck's definition of *ḥesed* must be extended, for those united in a common religion were expected to show *ḥesed*.

Ḥesed as a divine quality occurs fifteen times in prophetic writings, and of the pre-Exilic references all but Jer. 9:23 and 31:3 are questionable as to genuineness. The early prophets, emphasizing impending national doom, did not make *ḥesed* part of their message. After the fall of Jerusalem an appeal is made to the divine *ḥesed*, particularly in II Isaiah, thus the glosses in the writings of the earlier prophets were probably inserted after the year 586.[6] *Ḥesed* as a human quality does appear in Hos. 4:1; 6:4, 6; 10:12, and 12:7 (a non-Hoseanic passage), in Mic. 6:8, and Zech. 7:9.

In Jer. 31:3 Bowen finds a new element entering the concept of divine *ḥesed*. He disagrees with Glueck that forgiveness is to be found in Exod. 34:6 f., arguing that here *ḥesed* is reserved for those who have been steadfastly faithful rather than for repenting sinners. When God's *ḥesed* is associated with forgiveness the concept rests upon a basis deeper than covenant, for Yahweh morally could not withdraw his *ḥesed* from sinful Israel (cf. Jer. 16:5), therefore *ḥesed*

[6] *Ibid.*, pp. 135 f.

becomes "grace," "loving-kindness," and approaches "love." The Deuteronomist had stressed love for God on the part of man as a condition on which the divine *ḥesed* was extended, but in Jeremiah something new has been introduced.

References to *ḥesed* in Wisdom literature are limited to Job and Proverbs. Job has little to offer, for 10:12 is a textual error, 37:13 belongs to the Elihu speeches which are generally recognized as intrusions, and 6:14 has to do with social *ḥesed* and contributes nothing new. Apart from the exception in Prov. 14:22 where *ḥesed* constitutes a reward for goodness, Bowen, arguing that Proverbs has nothing to say about the kingdom of God and that *ḥesed* here is "a social virtue which one may profitably show toward all men," qualifies Glueck's conclusions.[7]

Within late historical writings Bowen finds *ḥesed* used five times as a human quality and fifteen times as an attribute of God, six of these depending upon earlier sources. The Chronicler accepted the Deuteronomic view that the Davidic dynasty would be preserved through God's covenantal loyalty and divine *ḥesed*. Through God's *ḥesed* a Jew could gain favor in the sight of a foreign potentate. God's *ḥesed* might be earned through zealous service on behalf of the Sabbath. As a human quality *ḥesed* has the force of reciprocal kindness and may be related to zeal for worship, the law or institutions of religion, and such cultic *ḥesed* could be rewarded with divine blessing.

Ḥesed, Bowen notes, appears in the Psalter over 100 times,[8] generally with reference to times of personal or national affliction. Nine Psalms emphasize God's *ḥesed* as a prudent act lest Yahweh be regarded as impotent (6:5; 13:6; 40:11, 12; 44:27; 88:12; 90:14; 94:18; 109:21, 22; 115:1) thus making an appeal to God's self-interest. Other passages, such as Ps. 25:6, 7; 106:1, 7, 45; 107:1, 8, 15, 21, 31; 138:8, suggest that Yahweh show *ḥesed* as a moral imperative to a distressed people or else fall short of moral responsibilities. Five psalms emphasize Yahweh's universal interest so that his *ḥesed* is of benefit to all as it is revealed in "cosmical forces."[9] Yahweh is described as creator and sustainer of the universe but his *ḥesed* is limited to his own people (cf. Ps. 33:5–9; 36:6–8; 147:8–10) except in Ps. 117:1 where an exception occurs and the invitation is given to all people to worship Yahweh and share in the benefits of his *ḥesed*,

[7] Cf. Glueck, pp. 27 f. (German), p. 61 f. (English).

[8] Bowen, *op. cit.*, pp. 322 f.

[9] *Ibid.*, p. 325. Cf. Pss. 33, 36, 103, 117, 147.

thus transcending the *gemeinschaftsgemässe Verhaltungsweise.* Bowen admits that his interpretation of this last Psalm is open to question even as he complains that Glueck has omitted the universalistic overtones of the Psalm. In Jonah 4:2, Ruth 1:8, and II Sam. 15:20 parallel universalistic emphases are found. Another group of Psalms demonstrates that divine *ḥesed* is linked to worship. Ps. 5:8 and 23:6 suggest that through Yahweh's *ḥesed* worship is made satisfying to the worshipper, and Ps. 66:19 f. indicates that through worship one gains access to Yahweh's *ḥesed.* In Ps. 48:10; 63:4 f.; 92:3 the very occasion for giving praise and thanksgiving is Yahweh's expression of *ḥesed.*

Bowen's major point of difference with Glueck is in methodology for he believes that by adopting the literary-critical techniques he can point up significant aspects of *ḥesed* not covered by Glueck. For example, he finds that with the Chronicler *ḥesed* loses the rich ethical-religion conception it held for prophets and sages, and becomes identified with zealous activity on behalf of the temple, the priesthood, and the cultus.[10] He believes that his method demonstrates that the Deuteronomists began to condition Yahweh's responsibility to show *ḥesed* upon the moral and religious integrity of the prospective recipient. Forgiveness as an expression of divine *ḥesed* is a conspicuous emphasis, Bowen finds, and may represent an original contribution of late prophetic writers.

The derivative term *ḥasid* which may, like *ḥesed,* be applied to both God and man conveys no basic ideas not contained in *ḥesed.* Bowen notes that *ḥasid* may be used with reference to outstanding persons in Israel's history such as Moses (Deut. 33:8); or Nathan (by allusion in Ps. 89:2, cf. II Sam. 7:17), or one of high ethical or religious attainment (II Sam. 22:26; Ps. 18:26; 86:2; 141:5), a man of prayer, faithful to Yahweh (Ps. 4:4; 16:10; 32:6). The *ḥasidim* could be the nation Israel (Ps. 50:5; 148:14; 149:1, 5, 9), worshippers of Yahweh (Ps. 30:5; 145:10), or, more often, those characterized by moral character and religious zeal (Ps. 31:24; 37:28; 43:1, etc.). The *hasidaioi* of I Macc. 2:41; 7:12–14; II Macc. 14:6 are zealots for the law and are to be distinguished from the *ḥasidim* despite the philological relationship.

Ludwig Köhler, discussing *zebaḥ,* communion sacrifice, noted that participation in a sacrificial meal creates an alliance, a relationship of reciprocal obligations of *ḥesed wᵉʾemet.*[11] He comments "Nelson

[10] *Ibid.*, p. 425.

[11] Ludwig Köhler, *Theologie des Alten Testaments* (Tübingen: J. C. B. Mohr,

Glueck . . . has shown that חֶסֶד also means 'solidarity' and חֶסֶד וֶאֱמֶת therefore 'reliable solidarity,'" and W. F. Lofthouse . . . "has confirmed it."[12]

Shortly afterward Walther Eichrodt also drew upon Glueck's research. For Eichrodt the covenant concept is basic for the understanding of the relationship between God and Israel and he writes "it can be demonstrated that the covenant-union between Yahweh and Israel is an original element in all sources, despite their being in fragmentary form."[13] Israel's covenant relationship with God assimilated ideas associated with human covenants and "wherever a *b^erit* governs relations between human beings, the kind of behavior which is expected in the normal way of those so associated is clearly recognized as *ḥesed*."[14] Glueck, he notes, has demonstrated that *ḥesed* constitutes "the proper object of a *b^erit* and may almost be described as its content. The possibility of the establishment and maintenance of a covenant rests on the practice of *ḥesed*."[15] The conduct of those bound in a covenant was characterized by loyal mutual service, and Yahweh could be expected to render kindness and succor, and even punishment where punishment could be conceived of as the instrument to restore covenant relationships. The unbreakable constancy of Yahweh's *ḥesed* is reflected in the conjunction of the words *ʾemet* and *ḥesed* and in the use of *ḥesed ʾelohim* and *ḥesed Yahweh* to describe outstanding examples of human devotion and loyalty such as in II Sam. 9:3 where David wishes to show loyalty to Saul's family, or in I Sam. 20:14 with reference to the Jonathan-David friendship. Such constancy, in some respects similar to that found in Babylonian and Sumerian descriptions of divine-human relationships, is to be differentiated in view of the association of Yahweh's *ḥesed* with the covenantal pattern, for in the covenant relationship *ḥesed* is given a much sounder base.[16] Further strength was afforded the Hebrew relationship in the worship of a single deity in contrast to the polytheistic pattern of Mesopotamia. In prophetic writings Eichrodt sees a transformation of the *ḥesed* concept making it without parallel

1935); Ludwig Köhler, *Old Testament Theology*, trans. A. S. Todd (English ed., based on 3rd rev. ed. of 1953; Philadelphia: Westminster Press, 1957), p. 183.

[12] *Ibid.*, p. 250, n. 148.

[13] Walther Eichrodt, *Theologie des Alten Testaments* (Leipzig: J. C. Hinrichs, 1939). Walther Eichrodt, *Theology of the Old Testament*, trans. J. A. Baker (based on the 6th German ed. of 1959; Philadelphia: Westminster Press, 1961), I, 36.

[14] *Ibid.*, p. 232.

[15] Quoting Glueck: p. 13 (German), p. 47 (English).

[16] *Ibid.*, p. 235.

anywhere in the ancient near east. The relationship which Yahweh threatens to withdraw consists of *ḥesed* and *raḥamim* — loving kindness and mercy — so that if the sinner is repentant the old limitations of *ḥesed* are transcended by *raḥamim* and Yahweh receives the *ḥasid* — just as Hosea received Gomer — to bestow eternal *ḥesed*. Thus "what began as *ḥesed* granted as a matter of course in the *b^erit* has become, as a result of the thoroughgoing questioning of the old conception, a completely new concept of faithfulness and love. The miraculous quality of this new love is seen to reside not only in the condescension of the exalted God, but also, much more inwardly, in the mystery of the divine will which seeks communion with man."[17] With the deepening of the *ḥesed* concept Eichrodt finds a simultaneous broadening of the scope of *ḥesed* so that creation itself is embraced, and *ḥesed* is made to signify the "most profound meaning of the relationship between Creator and creature."[18] Thus the Psalmist could speak of the whole earth being full of Yahweh's *ḥesed* (Ps. 33:5; 119:64). Although this universalistic concept was more rationalistic it was not constantly maintained, and it lacked something of the warmth of the *ḥesed* concept of the prophets.

The essay by B. D. Eerdmans, one of several studies devoted to the *ḥasidim*, makes only passing reference to *ḥesed*.[19] *Ḥesed*, he noted, in the substantive form can refer to the "goodwill" of God (Exod. 34:7), of kings (I Kings 20:31), or of men (Prov. 11:17) and like *ḥen* ("favor") indicates the attitude of superiors to inferiors or equals. The *ḥasidim* are to be recognized as erudite laymen, intimately acquainted with the historical traditions of Israel, who, like the prophets, spoke against the evil they saw in their society. Great emphasis was placed upon confessions of faith but the importance of sacrifice was also recognized (cf. Ps. 50:14, 23; 69:31). The *ḥasidim* were capable of playing instruments and composing psalms.

Eerdmans stated that while every *ḥasid* had to be righteous not every righteous man was a *ḥasid*. A number of passages mention the *ḥasidim* together with the "perfect" (תמים), the "upright" (ישר), the "righteous" (צדיק), (cf. Prov. 2:7; Ps. 18:26; 97:10–12; Mic. 7:2). The *ḥasid* trusted in God (cf. Ps. 32:7) for he knew that God has set the *ḥasidim* apart for himself (Ps. 4:4, reading *ḥasid* for *ḥesed*) and that they were related to God through a special covenant so that God and the *ḥasidim* stood on one side, the people on the other (cf.

[17] *Ibid.*, pp. 238 f. [18] *Ibid.*, p. 239.

[19] B. D. Eerdmans, "The Chasidim," *Oudtestamentische Studien* (Leiden: E. J. Brill, 1942), I, 176–257.

Ps. 50:5; 16:1–11). They were the defenders of Yahweh's cause (Ps. 79:1–3) and stood as a special group associated with priests II Chron. 6:41 f.; Ps. 132:16) and people (Ps. 85:9) but not necessarily identified with these groups (Ps. 148:14). They believed they were given an exceptional role (Ps. 18:5–6; 37:28; 52:11; 89:20; 97:10; 116; Prov. 2:8) for even the Levite holding the Urim and Thummim was a *ḥasid* (Deut. 33:8–11).

This exceptional group, whose pledge is preserved in Ps. 149, a strict fanatical band in pre-Exilic times, with diminished influence in the Persian period, ultimately united with the Maccabees (cf. I Macc. 2:42–44).

The studies in *ḥesed* by Norman Snaith present conclusions very much like those of Glueck although Glueck's work is not mentioned. In 1944 Snaith, in drawing a distinction between *ḥesed* and *ʾahavah*, wrote that both mean "love," but *ḥesed*, "in all its varied shades of meaning, is conditional upon there being a covenant."[20] "Without the prior existence of a covenant, there never could be any *ḥesed* at all."[21] *ʾAhavah* refers to unconditional love, or what Snaith calls "God's election love," *ḥesed* to "covenant love."

In analyzing the etymology of *ḥesed* Snaith noted that in Lev. 20:17 and in Prov. 14:34 *ḥesed* refers to "shame" or "reproach" or "defilement," and in Prov. 25:10 the corresponding verb form has the same significance. Elsewhere the very opposite meaning — "love" — is reflected. Snaith rejected the proposal of W. Robertson Smith which had been accepted in the Brown, Driver, Briggs lexicon that two separate roots are involved, one related to the Arabic *ḥašada* meaning "to assemble," with reference to the hospitality due to a guest from which the term *ḥesed* comes, the other, *ḥašada*, meaning "envy." Although the Arabic *shin* may be equated with the Hebrew *samek* the equation is rare. Snaith preferred Gesenius' suggestion that the primary meaning of *ḥesed* was "keenness," or "ardent zeal," and that the word developed along two lines — one revealing itself in love and kindness toward a person, and the other in emulation ending in envy or ambition. Snaith suggested that the "bad" meanings in Hebrew are due to Aramaic influence, and the "good" meaning in Aramaic and Syriac are due to the influence of Hebrew.

Ḥesed, Snaith found, denotes attitudes of loyalty and faithfulness which should be observed by both parties in a covenant. The "leal-

[20] Norman H. Snaith, *The Distinctive Ideas of the Old Testament* (London: Epworth Press, 1944), p. 95.

[21] *Loc. cit.*

love" interpretation of George Adam Smith is acceptable only for early stages in the development of the *ḥesed* concept when the word is used of covenant in general. When *ḥesed* was applied to the divine covenant "it was realized by the prophets that such a covenant could be maintained only by that persistent, determined, steadfast love of God." The term, therefore, involves faithfulness rather than kindness, for in almost every case *ḥesed* reveals a sub-stratum of fixed, determined, almost stubborn steadfastness. Snaith prefers "faithfulness" to "kindness" as a single term to translate *ḥesed*, but suggests that the best translation is "sure-love" or "covenant love." If *ḥesed* can stand for God's sure-love, then *ḥasid* must mean an individual's sure-love for another. Because Israel's *ḥesed* involved knowledge of God, loyalty expressed in terms of true worship and proper human behavior, then *ḥasid* refers to the loyalty of the faithful, and in post-Exilic times came to refer to pious devotion and loyalty to the law.

In a later study of "loving-kindness" Snaith defined *ḥesed* as "the steady, persistent refusal of God to wash his hands of wayward Israel."[22] The maintenance of God's covenant with his wayward people underscored the significance of divine mercy, so that from the third century onward, translators used the Greek word *eleos* — mercy, pity — as a translation of *ḥesed*.

H. Wheeler Robinson, who also failed to mention Glueck's research, agreed with Kautzsch that *ḥesed* was derived from a fundamental concept of conformity to justice within a norm within juristic, ethical, and theocratic realms.[23] *Ḥesed*, the outstanding word used to describe the content of divine-human relations, may often be rendered "grace," but "grace" fails to suggest "the element of loyalty, or moral obligation, of social bond which the Hebrew word includes, an element finding parallel expression in the quite different word translated 'redeemer,' properly 'kinsman-vindicator.' "[24]

The root meaning of *ḥesed* Robinson argued, was effectively brought out in the Arabic equivalent signifying "promptitude to help," or in the verb form "to gather with a view to help." Thus *ḥesed* referred to a deep-seated relationship between God and Israel constituting God's righteousness carried into effect and designed to rouse a sense of repentance in man. In the human realm *ḥesed* signified "loyal helpfulness," and was one of two moral virtues, the other

[22] Norman H. Snaith, "Loving-kindness" in *A Theological Word Book of the Bible*, ed. Alan Richardson (New York: Macmillan, 1951), pp. 136–7.

[23] H. Wheeler Robinson, *Inspiration and Revelation in the Old Testament* (Oxford, 1964).

[24] *Ibid.*, p. 57.

being *mishpaṭ*. *Mishpaṭ* used in a concrete sense was the decision of a judge who tried a case and passed sentence distinguishing between innocence and guilt and rendering *mishpaṭ* as that due everyman. *Ḥesed*, a complementary moral virtue, involved an element of moral obligation, the recognition of a social bond which demands mutual helpfulness even beyond the requirements of justice and reflected the "spontaneous expression of an inner spirit or disposition."[25] These terms reflect nomadic origins where survival depended upon social solidarity. *Ḥesed* in God is human *ḥesed* "raised to new powers and unexpected applications" and means the bond of helpfulness uniting God to man so that it could be said that God would not hold his anger forever, and is unfailing. Psalm 36 is the psalm of God's *ḥesed*. In an abstract sense *mishpaṭ* also is an attribute of God and thus is an attribute of a man who conforms to God's nature.

Convinced that earlier research into the meaning of *ḥesed* gave scant attention to Latin and Greek translations of the term, and paid little heed to exegetical studies prior to the nineteenth century, Felix Asensio undertook a new investigation including an analysis of *ʾemet* which often appears together with *ḥesed* in the phrase *ḥesed wᵉʾemet*.[26] Asensio moved away from what he deemed to be a rigid one-sided emphasis, away from the legalistic or duty-obligation interpretation of Glueck, to stress "mercy-feeling," and "mercy-work." Glueck had recognized these implications of *ḥesed* in the analysis of Num. 14:19, but Asensio made the element of divine grace the central feature of his analysis.

From the very start, when he began the study of the relationship of *ḥesed* to like terms in cognate languages, Asensio disagreed with Glueck. Rejecting the "striking parallel" which Glueck found in the Arabic, Asensio underscored the double meaning ("germinate" and "gather together") of the Arabic, reflected also in Aramaic and perhaps in the Syriac *ḥesda*. He would argue that no definite solution has been found to explain the dual interpretation afforded by the term.[27]

In a study of the LXX translations of *ḥesed* Asensio[28] points out that ἔλεος the word used predominantly to translate *ḥesed* not only answers to the sense of beneficence and goodness of the Hebrew term,

[25] *Ibid.*, p. 85.

[26] Felix Asensio, *Misericordia et Veritas, el Ḥesed y ʾEmet divinos, su influjo religioso-social en la historia de Israel* (Rome: Apud Aedes Universitatis Gregorianae, 1949).

[27] *Ibid.*, pp. 32 ff.

[28] *Ibid.*, pp. 37 ff.

but moves from internal feelings to external manifestations of these sentiments. The occasional use of *δικαιοσύνη* for *ḥesed* as well as for *ʾemet* points up the recognition by the Alexandrian translators of an indirect relationship between these two terms.

The usual translation of *ḥesed* in Latin is *misericordia* but on occasion *gratia*, *miseror*, *misereor*, *miserationes*, *clemens*, and *clementia* may be used.[29] In Gen. 19:19; 47:29 *ḥesed-ḥen* is translated by *gratia-misericordia*, or, in Gen. 39:21, by *gratia-miserari*. In Ruth 1:8; 2:20; 3:10 the translation of *ḥesed* moves from *misericordia* to *gratia* and back to *misericordia*. Thus *misericordia* follows the pattern of the Greek *eleos* moving from feelings or sentiment to the actualization of these feelings. In the few passages where the plural *miserationes* is substituted for the plural *misericordiae* the significance is that of fulfilled favors or blessings rather than sentiment or internal feeling (cf. Gen. 32:11; Isa. 63:7). The substitution of *clementia* in Proverbs for *misericordia* is not so clear.

The term *ḥasid* in its plural form *ḥasidim*, while immediately calling to mind the *Hasidaioi* of I Macc. 2:42; 7:13, and II Macc. 14:6, finds no support for interpretation as a community in pre-Maccabaean texts.[30] *Ḥasid* has an active sense in the idea that God is *ḥasid* to man, and man is *ḥasid* to his fellow man. God's *ḥasid* is compassionate (cf. Jer. 3:12) and although man's *ḥasid* is related to the practise of justice, equity, and love in social life and tends to be ended with the completion of the act, it too may contain compassion. Used in relationship of man to God, *ḥasid* has a double movement: the movement of man towards God, and the movement of God toward man. The term is thus related to the religious life of man.

The study of the phrase עשה חסד provides no distinction between the content of divine and human *ḥesed* (unless it be in divine perfection) and, Asensio finds, has nothing to do with obligation in the strict sense. If an obligatory element does appear it is to be found in conjunction with an oath or some similar circumstance. The fundamental meaning of *ḥesed* as the object of the verb is that of spontaneous and free favor, mercy-work which always presupposes and at times includes mercy-sentiment and affection. Nor does Asensio find anything to alter his conclusions in his study of the relationships existing between *ḥesed* and *raḥamim* or *ḥesed* and *ḥen*.[31]

The analysis of *ḥesed* in relation to words with which it is associated led Asensio to the conclusion that the term signified divine

[29] *Ibid.*, pp. 57 ff.
[30] *Ibid.*, pp. 49 f.
[31] *Ibid.*, pp. 118 f.

goodness, the internal spontaneous compassion marked with forgiveness and the continual doing of good. As in the human realm the inner feeling must be expressed through action, any attempt to limit *ḥesed* to pure sentiment is not fair to the term. Nevertheless *ḥesed* as presented in the formula base of the covenant is fundamentally merciful feeling or mercy-feeling (*misericordia-sentimento*) quick to become mercy work (*misericordia-obras*) in forgiveness and recognition of the covenant, a point recognized by Glueck in the discussion of Num. 14:19 (pp. 87–88) but, Asensio complains, ignored by him in the development of *ḥesed*.[32]

To substantiate his rejection of the obligatory sense that Glueck found in *ḥesed* Asensio traced the use of the term in the career of Abraham. The *ḥesed* shown by Sara to Abraham when she pretends to be his sister was not an obligatory act but rather a generous spontaneous proof of wifely love (cf. Gen. 12:13; 20:11–13). When Abimelech, king of Gerar sought from Abraham *ḥesed* like that which Abimelech had given, there was no obligation on Abraham's part to accept the request. However, once the *ḥesed* was agreed to and the relationship sealed with an oath, *ḥesed* became obligatory. The divine *ḥesed* referred to by Eleazer, servant of Abraham signified continued divine favors (Gen. 24). Nor was the response of Abraham's cousin to the request for Rebecca as a bride for Isaac based on obligatory *ḥesed* but was a response to the recognition of divine intervention in the matter (Gen. 24:49–51).[33]

Nor does Asensio find any sense of duty, obligation or rights but rather beneficence and favor involved in the story of Rahab's salvation (Josh. 2:12–14), in the sparing of the man of Bethel by the house of Joseph (Judg. 1:24), or in Joseph's request of the cup-bearer (Gen. 40:14–15). The same can be said of the *ḥesed* of Gen. 39:21–22, Ezra 7:27–38; 9:9 and Neh. 1:11. The *ḥesed* which David offers to Jonathan's crippled son Mephiboset demonstrates a gracious heart although David's pact with Jonathan (I Sam. 20:4–17, 42) may be involved. The *ḥesed* shown by the people of Jabesh-gilead to the dead Saul reflects love not justice, graciousness and generosity rather than obligation (II Sam. 2:5–6). However, Asensio has recognized the obligatory note that appears in the use of *ḥesed* in the Book of Nehemiah, as well as arising out of association with *bᵉrit* and *ʾemet*.[34]

In discussing *ḥesed* as an essential element in the history of Israel,

[32] *Ibid.*, pp. 71 f.
[33] *Ibid.*, pp. 89 ff.
[34] *Ibid.*

Asensio began with the Sinai covenant, the overriding concept in Israelite religion and discovered that the divine goodness as expressed against a background of sin in Exodus had the sense of divine compassion, forgiving, forgetting, and following with beneficent love. This is clear in the repetition of the first promulgation (Exod. 20) in Exodus 34 following the golden calf episode where the formula "to do *ḥesed*" is repeated with the following expansion: the addition of the phrase *el raḥum*, the juxtaposition of *ʾemet* and *ḥesed*, and the union of the two terms with *el* as genitives of quality. The Sinaitic formula is repeated, often in essence, in poetic, historical, and prophetic writings (cf. Ps. 86; 103:8; 145:8; Joel 2:13; Jonah 4:2; Jer. 9:23).

The divine *ḥesed* incorporated in the promises to the patriarchs is made firm in David (cf. II Sam. 7:15; I Chron. 17:13). The *ḥesed* which appears as mercy-feeling toward David has its fulfillment in mercy-work. The ongoing nature of David's reign is guaranteed, with David's son forming the first link in the chain. One can thus speak of the *ḥesed* of contracted obligation, but *ḥesed* and obligation are two different things which may be joined together when the given promise is converted into a duty, in which case *ḥesed* is neither simply a promise nor goodness, but goodness or favor sealed with a promise. Isa. 55:3 describing the new Jerusalem, promised an eternal covenant fulfilling the reliable *ḥesed* of David. This same Davidic-messianic inference Asensio found implied in Isa. 63:7. Extending his discussion to Ps. 89, Asensio suggested that Glueck, while not postulating a parallelism between *b^erit* and *ḥesed*, implied it. But, he has written, *ḥesed* must not be confused with the oath that confirms it and converts it into obligation. *Ḥesed* comprised the content of the oath.[35]

The Psalmists recognized the miracle of divine goodness, an element of God's *ḥesed* extending beyond the sin and apostasy of Israel (Pss. 106:1, 7; 107:1).[36] Because the *ḥesed* stands in close relationships with *raḥamim* and *s^eliḥah* the position of those who deny the meaning of gift, grace, benevolence to *ḥesed* is untenable.[37] The concept of *ḥesed* set forth in the Sinaitic formula with the emphasis on generosity and dynamic love was maintained in Psalms depicting the atmosphere of battle (Ps. 18, 59, 62, 80, 144).

The formula in Jer. 33:10–11

כי־טוב יהוה
כי־לעולם חסדו

[35] *Ibid.*, pp. 109 ff.
[36] *Ibid.*, p. 137.
[37] *Ibid.*, p. 164.

reached back, Asensio stated, to Davidic times and was preserved by temple singers and musicians whose function it was to keep alive through music the recognition of the generous gifts of God in the past and to project the hope of these blessings into the future (cf. I Chron. 16:8–36; II Chron. 5:13; 7:3–6; Ps. 100:3–5; 106:1, 2, 4, 21–22, 45; 107:1, 8, 15, 21, 31, 41; 118:1, 29; 136:1).[38] The paralleling of *ᵓemet* and *ḥesed* gave to the projected *ḥesed* the assurance of Yahweh's fidelity and reliability.

Despite particularistic and nationalistic emphases within the Psalms implicit overtones of universalism can be found.[39] For example, Ps. 100 introduces the liturgical formula to the non-Israelite world (cf. also Isa. 56:6–7; Ps. 104:27; 136:4–9, 25–26; 145:7–9, 15–17, 21). The nationalistic elements are never lost, but Asensio prefers to see in nationalistic Israel a type of the universalistic Israel of the new covenant by which the divine *ḥesed* was made to surpass the limits which nationalistic emphases appear to have imposed.

In 1952 Hans Joachim Stoebe published a report of his dissertation on *ḥesed*.[40] Stoebe's primary assumption was that true synonyms do not exist in a language, but each term has its own distinctive range of meaning which may be partially ascertained by examining terms with which the word is associated, discerning, of course, the scope of meaning of each parallel term. The aging of a language tends to blur sharp distinctions.

Stoebe first examined the relationship of *ḥesed* to *ḥen* and *raḥamim* and noted that *ḥesed* never stands next to *ḥen* (in Gen. 19:19; 39:21; 47:29 the terms are clearly separated, but in Esther 2:17, a late source, the distinctive characteristics are not clear), but often next to *raḥamim*. Nor does *ḥen* ever stand next to *raḥamim* in the nominal form but only in adjectival and verbal forms. When *ḥesed* and *raḥamim* appear together, *ḥesed* always stands first (Jer. 16:5; Hos. 2:21; Zech. 7:9; Ps. 103:4).

The stem *ḥn* means as a verb and a noun the granting or demonstration of favor with emphasis focused not only upon the free good-will of him who shows *ḥen* but also upon the recipient. The demonstration of grace or favor often included an answer to a situation (II Sam. 12:22; Amos 5:15; Isa. 30:19; 33:2; Mal. 1:9; Ps. 4:2; 26:11; 27:7; 30:11; 57:2; 86:3; 119:58), or the recognition of un-

[38] *Ibid.*, pp. 170–73.

[39] *Ibid.*, p. 181.

[40] Hans Joachim Stoebe, "Die Bedeutung des Wortes Häsäd im Alten Testament," *Vetus Testamentum*, 1952, pp. 244–54.

fortunate circumstances (Exod. 22:26; Ps. 6:3; 25:16; 31:10; 56:2; 123:3; Job 19:21) which may have been partly alluded to in the petition for *ḥnn* introduced by the particle *ki.* It would appear that at times *ʾānah* could stand for *ḥānan.* Objective regulations on the noun *ḥen* are rare and when they occur are always brought into relation to the object of a demonstration of *ḥen,* never to the subject. When the meaning is strongly transferred to the object the noun takes on the meaning of "grace." In the reflexive form the verb means "to request someone's favor for oneself."

In contrast to *ḥen, raḥamim* was oriented toward the subject of the demonstration of goodwill and indicates specific acts of pity or mercy. The term does not appear as the subject in expressions of faith for only infrequently was it made the standard of a prayer or act (cf. Isa. 63:7; Neh. 9:27–8 for exceptions). Strain or tension appears to be associated with the intrinsic meaning of the term and at one time *raḥamim* means an emotionally-toned warm-hearted action not expressed in accordance with the will (I Kings 3:26; Lam. 4:10), and at another an action of the mind leading to concrete expression (Deut. 13:18; I Kings 8:50; Jer. 42:12). In the verbal form *rḥm* defines only a masculine area, but the nominal form is used of both men and women and its sense is to be determined according to which sex is meant. Whenever *raḥamim* means the restoration of communal relationships it includes the idea of forgiveness. (Deut. 13:18; I Kings 8:5; Jer. 42:2; Mic. 7:19; Ps. 51:3; 79:8; Dan. 9:9; Prov. 28:13.)

Like *raḥamim, ḥesed* is oriented solely toward the subject of the expression of kindness. Both singular and plural forms are to be found, with the plural limited to Exilic and post-Exilic periods. Only in the singular is *ḥesed* a measure of behavior or the subject of confidence or trust. In the plural the scope of meaning of the term is restricted and, like *raḥamim, ḥesed* now means the concrete demonstration of a benevolent attitude. *Ṭuv/ṭov* join *ḥesed* or take its place (Isa. 63:7; Ps. 69:17; 106:1; 107:1; 118:29; 136:1). Stoebe has suggested that the original meaning of *ḥesed* was goodness and affability, and that *raḥamim* exerted a limiting effect upon *ḥesed.*

In an exegetical study Stoebe found that the uses of *ḥesed* in Judges through Kings make it clear that the term was common in profane speech and depicted an attitude or aspect of human behavior. Judging by the limited references, the term played a less significant role in describing the attitude of God toward man (II Sam. 2:6; II Sam. 15:20; II Sam. 7:15; I Kings 3:6). *Ḥesed* expressed a goodness or friendliness going beyond that which one normally had the right to expect, beyond that which was deserved, and described an action based in a magnanimous readiness to act for another. Through such action community becomes possible.

In early Wisdom literature the same profane usage of *ḥesed* is found, (Prov. 11:17; 19:22; 20:6; 21:21; 31:26; Job 6:14). In later literature in religious settings the term indicates the attitude of God toward man (Ecclus. 47:22; 50:24; 51:3, 8) and human devoutness (Ecclus. 40:17; 41:11; 43:33; 44:1, 10; 46:7; 49:3). The same duality of meaning is found in J (E sources are too scanty to permit formation of conclusions) with some passages describing the attitude of men to one another (Gen. 24:49; 47:29; Josh. 2:12) and others referring to God's relationship to men (Gen. 24:12, 14, 27; 32:11; 39:21).

Stoebe pressed his analysis through the two versions of the Decalogue (Exod. 20 labelled "E" because it constitutes a late formulation, and Exod. 34, "J"). In the "E" formulation God is called *ᵓel kannaᵓ* (20:5) and the threat of punishment stands foremost. The unconditional promise of grace follows in vs. 6 and is not consistent with the essence of *ḥesed*. In J the proclamation of a God as *ᵓel raḥum wᵉḥannun ᵓerekh ᵓappayim wᵉrav ḥesed wᵉᵓemet* the promise of grace is foremost and the promise of punishment motivated by the phrase "and will by no means clear the guilty" of verse 7 stands as an attachment. Stoebe suggested that here God's *ḥesed* rather than representing something basic in the divine nature serves as an extension of J's theology and as a setting for a liturgical formula stating something about God which could not be stipulated through familiar concepts. God's *ḥesed* is revealed in miracles (Exod. 34:10) and is the presupposition of the covenant (Exod. 34:9, 10). The relationship between *bᵉrit* and *ḥesed* is given stronger expression in the Deuteronomic writings, and the formula of Deut. 7:9 stands between Exod. 20 and 34 according to Stoebe. The significance of the covenant concept for the Deuteronomists is demonstrated by placing *bᵉrit* before *ḥesed*. As Deut. 7:9 appears to be a summarizing statement of the preceding verse which contains the words *ᵓahavāh* and *šᵉvuᶜāh*, then *bᵉrit* must be related to *šᵉvuᶜāh* and *ḥesed* to *ᵓahavāh*, which effects no essential change in the meaning of *ḥesed*.

Hosea adds a new element and describes the attitude of man toward God as *ḥesed*. God gave *ḥesed* to the people as a wedding gift (Hos. 2:21; 10:12) and thus began the community relationship (Hos. 2:22). God can expect from man the same *ḥesed*, manifested in human relationships (Hos. 4:1; 6:4, 6). The same double meaning of *ḥesed* can be found in Jeremiah. *Ḥesed* is what God does and gives (Jer. 9:9, 23; 15:5; 31:3) and what God expects of man (Jer. 9:23). The concept of *ḥesed* underlies Jeremiah's statement about the new covenant of the heart.

In Isa. 40–66 the word limitations of *ḥesed* are obscured as indicated by the use of the plural form (Isa. 55:3; 63:7) but clarified by the word *ᶜolām* (Isa. 54:8). With this new addition, Stoebe suggested, *ḥesed* approaches *bᵉrit*, and in later liturgical development of this union it appears that *bᵉrit* lost its meaning as a term referring to a one-time historical event and through extension of meaning was brought closer to *ḥesed*.

In the Psalms *ḥesed* is used primarily to designate divine characteristics, but because the term appears in the context of expressions of personal piety as well as in liturgical formulae a clear exposition is impossible. Stoebe suggests some of the songs may have undergone change through adaption in congregational usage to new insights. In lament Psalms, the *ḥesed* of God appears as a motif of the trust of the worshipper (Ps. 13:6, cf. 52:10 a thanksgiving song, and in a broader sense 21:8, 32:10), but trust may also be centered in the worshipper's good behavior (Ps. 7:9–11, 17; 11:2, 3, 5, 7; 54:7; 109:6 f.; 140:14). On occasion these two mutually exclusive factors are found together (Ps. 26:1, 3). The covenant concept plays a minor role and only occasional references are found (Ps. 25:10; 44:18; 74:20). Stoebe concludes that *ḥesed*, in Psalms of lament, is to be understood as a way of characterizing God and means essentially goodness and affability, so that the worshipper may trust in God's *ḥesed* as he trusts in God Himself (Ps. 22:5, 6; 25:2; 26:1; 31:7, 15; 56:5, 12).

There are signs which suggest that *ḥesed* tended to lose strength in its course of development, for the prayer for help is linked with the divine *ḥesed* (Ps. 25:7; 51:3; 69:17; 109:26; 119:88, 124, 149, 159), and the formula *lᵉmaᶜan ḥesed yahweh* (Ps. 6:5; 44:27) becomes parallel to *lᵉmaᵃᶜan šem yahweh* (Isa. 48:9; Jer. 14:7, 21; Ezek. 20:9, 14, 22, 44; Ps. 25:11; 31:4; 79:9; 109:21; 143:11). In addition the meaning of *ḥesed* at times shifts toward *raḥamim* and *ṭuv* (Ps. 23:6; 25:6, 7; 109:21). The redemption phrases within the lament Psalms indicate that to experience salvation is to move more deeply within the sphere of the divine *ḥesed* (Ps. 6:5; 13:6; 17:7; 31:17, 22; 49:14; 85:8; 86:13; 109:21, 26).

Within liturgical and hymnic materials the use of *ḥesed* is even less uniform. *Ḥesed* is frequently associated with *ᵓemet*. At times miracles are stressed as revelations of this divine *ḥesed* rather than God's acts in history (Ps. 106:7; 107:8, 15, 21, 31). In Ps. 105 the covenant replaces *ḥesed*. Despite the blurring of limits of meaning of the term *ḥesed*, the word does appear in its old meaning (Ps. 33).

A study of *ḥasid* introduced no essential change in the *ḥesed* concept. The *ḥasid* is one to whom God has shown *ḥesed* and who has been drawn into the divine community. The favored one is simultaneously the active pious one (Ps. 18:26; 37:28; 97:10).

In a study "intended to be popular, not scientific," treating the Psalter "as a whole, written by one Primary Author," Dom Rembert Sorg studied *ḥesed* and *ḥasid* in the Psalms within a broader framework of the "Spirituality of the Psalms."[41] The primary meaning of *ḥesed*, translated in the New Latin Version by *misericordia*, "mercy," "pity," eighty-three times; by *gratia*, "grace," or "graciousness," thirty-two times; by *bonitas*, "goodness," seven times; by *clementia*, "clemency," and *pietas*, "piety," and *benignitas*, "kindness," once; is to be discerned in Ps. 102:8–18. Descriptive terms reflecting slowness to anger, propitiousness, sympathetic understanding, quickness to forgive, and eternal fidelity "refer to the fundamental Love, which God has for 'those who fear Him.' "[42] *Ḥesed*, Sorg believes, "is the Old Testament revelation of St. John's: 'God is Charity' (I John 4:16), inasmuch as this connotes God's own way of loving and the secret motive of all His thinking and willing and acting."[43] *Ḥesed* appears to correspond to the Greek *agape* and Latin *caritas* as contrasted to *eros* and *amor*, but the English terms "love" or "charity" are unsatisfactory translations for they include features of love not included in *ḥesed*.

Aspects of divine *ḥesed* which Sorg often relates to New Testament concepts can be discerned in the one hundred twenty-eight times where the word occurs in the Psalms. *Ḥesed* is eternal (Ps. 105:1; 106:1; 117; 135); characterized by fidelity (Ps. 84:11; 88; 137:8); immensity (Ps. 32:5; 35:6; 56:11; 102:11; 107:5); fullness (Ps. 35:6–11); and reveals God's beneficence and saving spirit (Ps. 6:5; 30:17; 50:3). Ps. 97:2–3 which "hails the saving quality of Ḥesed" is "the Liturgy's Christmas song to celebrate the birth of Jesus, which means Savior."[44] In addition the divine *ḥesed* is marked by humility of love "which stoops to equality with its beloved, and even to the lower self-abasement of the 'form of a slave' (Phil. 2:7)."[45] Consequently God showers his *ḥesed* upon the poor and humble

[41] Dom Rembert Sorg, *Hesed and Hasid in the Psalms* (St. Louis, Mo.: Pio Decimo Press, 1953), p. 53. We have followed Sorg and used the enumeration from the Roman Catholic Bible which from Psalm 9 to 146 is one less than the numbers in Jewish and Protestant versions.

[42] *Ibid.*, p. 10.

[43] *Ibid.*, p. 10.

[44] *Ibid.*, p. 18.

[45] *Ibid.*, p. 18.

(Pss. 67, 71). The omnipotent power and justice that mark God's *ḥesed* (Ps. 61:12 f.) make it possible for God to give victory to the weak and poor and to laugh at the futility of creature self-exaltation (Ps. 2; 36:13, etc.). Simultaneously God is quick to pardon (Ps. 29:6).

The "law of *ḥesed*" promulgated at Sinai (Exod. 20:5–6), mitigated under the prophets (Ezek. 19, Isa. 55:7) indicates that God shows *ḥesed* to those who love and serve him, and "outraged love" to sinners who hate him.[46] The law of *ḥesed* is, Sorg suggests, simply the law of love, through which God recompenses man according to his deeds (Ps. 17:21–28; 61:12; 146:11). Saints (*ḥasidim*), who may be Jews, as opposed to Gentiles, or a class within the Israelite community often labeled "poor" or "humble," are zealous in maintenance of Torah and rejoice in their assurance of God's *ḥesed* (Ps. 30:7, 8a; 56:9–11; 91:2–3; 100:1; 107:3–5). Sinners (*reshaᶜim*) deny God (Ps. 13, 52, 35:2–5); blaspheme God (Ps. 73:10, 18, 22); are enemies of God (Ps. 91:10; 20:9 ff.; 88:52); are hostile to the *ḥasidim* (Ps. 73:19); and are identified with the privileged and wealthy. Certain political differences are also discernible in Ps. 25 and 42 suggesting that the "saints" were unwilling to compromise with Gentile concepts and that they stood for a theocratic form of government with the Torah as the constitution, Psalm 118 as the national anthem, and Jerusalem as the political capital. The calls directed to God to curse the sinner are prayers (cf. Ps. 106:6, 13, 19, 28), which not only set forth the innocence of the psalmist (Ps. 25:1–12; 16:1–5; 43:1–23, etc.), but reflect "the psalmist's idealism respecting his personal obligations of holiness."[47] Sorg notes that the cursing Psalms are, and have been, sung with devotion within "Holy Mother Church," and are relived in the "anathemas and condemnations which she has uttered against heretics throughout history,"[48] justifiably so, because, Sorg argues, the psalmists' enemies "are truly sinners and enemies of God."

According to Sorg, in the "spiritual meaning" of the Psalms Jesus is the New Testament "Ḥasid," exemplifying complete devotion to God, incarnating *ḥesed*. Subsequently the "predestined members" of the church are the *ḥasidim*.

The relationship between *ḥen* and *ḥesed* previously explored by Lofthouse was re-examined by William L. Reed in a study of the Old Testament concept of "grace" — the term, which together with

[46] *Ibid.*, p. 23.

[47] *Ibid.*, p. 37.

[48] *Ibid.*, p. 37. He cites the Decree, Encyclical and Oath against modernism by Pius X as a modern example.

"favor" and "charm" is often used as a translation for *ḥen.*[49] Although *ḥen* and *ḥesed* are related they are by no means identical. *Ḥesed,* which Reed following Snaith translates as "covenant love," rests upon an existing bond between parties and has "a connotation of active goodness" which does not always characterize *ḥen.* "When covenant-love is evidenced by Yahweh or the gracious deed is performed by a fellow Hebrew it is because good will (*ḥen*) has been present."[50] In disagreement with Lofthouse Reed found that *ḥen* does not imply the relationship of a superior to an inferior, although it may be used where such differences of status are involved, but signifies the capacity in the superior or the individual for good will or mercy, provoking a similar attitude in others.

The authors of the Targum, Peshitta, and LXX did not find a sharp difference between *ḥen* and *ḥesed,* for in some instances the same Aramaic, Syriac, or Greek word was used to render both *ḥen* and *ḥesed,* although in other cases separate words were used. "It is clear," Reed concludes, "that the Hebrew word *ḥen* has important implications for Old Testament religion as a word which shows that God was considered capable of good will and mercy. It would also appear that his good will or favor was a basis for his covenant-love rather than being in opposition to it or distinct from it."[51]

C. H. Dodd has pointed out that in the translation of *ḥesed* by the writers of the LXX no single Greek term was utilized and different words appear in different places.[52] Normally *ḥesed* was translated by ἔλεος or ἐλεημοσύνη, ἐλεήμων or πολυελος whether *ḥesed* referred to God or man. ἔλεος and ἐλεημοσύνη were also used in the LXX for Hebrew terms derived from such roots as *ḥnn* "to show favor," *rḥm* "to have compassion." Once the translation οἴκτειρμα appears, and three times χάρις. (Esther and Ecclus.) Within the Pentateuch *ḥesed* is sometimes translated δικαιοσύνη indicating a kind of righteousness associated with living according to the Law. However, δικαιοσύνη and ἐλεημοσύνη are also used to translate צדק. Thus *ḥesed* becomes "the typical quality of the devout," and can naturally be "identified with righteousness" although outside of the Pentateuch "it is clear that the sense of 'kindness' predominated."

[49] William L. Reed, "Some Implications of *ḥen* for Old Testament Religion" *Journal of Biblical Literature,* LXXIII (1954), pp. 36–41.

[50] *Ibid.,* p. 38.

[51] *Ibid.,* p. 41.

[52] C. H. Dodd, *The Bible and the Greeks* (London: Hoddern and Stoughton, 1954), pp. 55–69.

The adjective *ḥasid* is translated by ἐλεήμων once when it refers to God, but when it refers to men, generally ὅσιος and once also as εὐλαβούμενος, and once as εὐσεβής. By using ὅσιος as a translation, the LXX writers assumed *ḥasid* to mean "pious," for in common usage the term seems to have referred to that sanctioned by divine law, so that the *ḥasidim* were those who conformed to the Law. But ὅσιος was used by the LXX translators for Hebrew words derived from the roots טהר "pure," ישר "upright," קדש "holy," תמם "integrity," and שלם "completeness," or "soundness." Thus the term contains nothing of the original meaning of *ḥesed* but suggests piety, devoutness, moral correctness.

Jaques Guillet[53] has written that despite the illusion that may be created by the LXX translation of *ḥesed* as ἔλεος, *ḥesed* is not a sentiment or feeling for someone, but involves a real sense of obligation or duty which imposes a requirement of specific action. Nor is any explicit pact a prerequisite for bringing *ḥesed* into being, but as Nelson Glueck has shown, *ḥesed* "designates the attitude which is in order among people united by some bond" — which may center in marriage or relationships of host-guest, master-servant, friendship, or spring from a debt of gratitude. As such, *ḥesed* constitutes a basic element of loyalty and trust in the moral structure of Israelite social life. The Book of Ruth is permeated with the *ḥesed* concept, according to Guillet, and the love expressed in this book is that of fidelity, the "calm and profound attachment of a loyal heart." The association of *ʾemet* with *ḥesed* stresses the solidity and reliability of the relationship represented by *ḥesed*, and the *ḥesed wᵉʾemet* formula moves from a description of noble and chivalrous fidelity in the human realm to the full embodiment of "this generous and loyal solidity, truth" in the God of Israel and the Covenant who promised *ḥesed* to the descendants of David (II Sam. 7:15). Thus *ḥesed* is a covenantal term, interchangeable with *bᵉrit*, signifying the community established between God and his people.

A Festschrift published by the Estonian Theological Society in Exile to honor Prof. Joh. Kopp included a posthumous study of *ḥesed* by Uku Masing.[54] Utilizing a sociological and linguistic approach Masing discussed the relationship of *ḥesed* to potlatch rituals, con-

[53] Jaques Guillet, *Themes Bibliques* (Paris: F. Aubier, 1954). English edition, *Themes of the Bible*, trans. by Albert J. LaMothe, Jr. (Notre Dame: Fides Publishers Association, 1960), pp. 36–40.

[54] Uku Masing, "Der Begriff *Ḥesed* im Alttestamentlichen Sprachgebrauch" *Charisteria Iohanni Kopp: Papers of the Estonian Theological Society in Exile #7* (Holmae: Nov. 9, 1954), pp. 29–63.

sulted cognate languages and engaged in an exegetical analysis of the biblical text. In addition to the "good" connotation of *ḥesed*, a bad meaning is found in the piᶜel form of the verb (cf. Prov. 25:10, Ecclus. 14:2), and in a few instances in late literature in the substantive form (Prov. 14:34; 28:22; Job 6:14; Lev. 20:17; Ecclus. 34:31). Masing associated the dual meanings with a hypothetical proto-Aramaic root *ḥsd* through which it came into Aramaic, Hebrew, and Arabic (it is not found in Akkadian), being introduced into Palestine by the invading tribes. An analysis of the interpretation of the Arabic *ḥasd*, which originally appears to have referred to a gathering in preparation for battle, led Masing to associate the term with potlatch rituals. In such a ritual a beneficent act might be regarded as a favor, or, should one be unable to reciprocate, as an insult. The one who demonstrated favor or *ḥsd* stood above the receiver. The stem *ḥsd* originally meant a definite action characteristic of a potlatch giver or similar person.

Masing rejected Nelson Glueck's analysis as "a talmudizing theory" (eine talmudisierende Theorie), failing to achieve clear distinctions between *ḥesed* and *ẓadik* and *ẓadikah*, for these terms also imply a society and a rule of conduct.[55] Nor did Masing accept the idea that involved in *ḥesed* was a pattern of mutual reciprocity, for he argued that the aid or favor given by an inferior to a superior was not designated as *ḥesed*. In Judg. 1:24; II Sam. 2:5; Judg. 8:35 *ḥesed* is demonstrated by sizeable groups to individuals. In Judg. 1:24 the action of the traitor is not designated as *ḥesed* to Israel, because in older literature one individual member of a large group may not show *ḥesed*. As the man's action is not labelled *ḥesed* the Israelite *ḥesed* cannot be interpreted as reciprocal action.[56] A hidden political connotation was discerned by Masing in II Sam. 2:5 in David's question "how can one to whom you must show *ḥesed* be king or master?," for to show *ḥesed* is to place oneself above another. David was treating Saul not as a king but as a *captatio benevolentiae* (stressing the importance of the Jabeshites), or as a relative who had been master of Jabesh. With regard to Judg. 8:35 Masing argued that if Gideon's action involved *ḥesed* and one was expected to respond in kind, why did the Israelites fail to do so? Because, Masing contended, the demonstration of *ḥesed* did not create obligations.

Gen. 40:14 demonstrates that he who sought *ḥesed* from another placed himself beneath that person, for when Joseph showed goodness to his captors it was not labelled *ḥesed*. Apart from II Chron. 24:22

[55] *Ibid.*, p. 45.

[56] *Ibid.*, p. 46.

and II Sam. 2:5 there is no reference in the Bible to a subject or vassal showing *ḥesed* to a king. In II Chron. 24:22 it is apparent, Masing reasoned, that the Chronicler valued the king less than the high priest and considered the monarch to be subordinate. Nor can II Sam. 3:8 be employed in this context, for Masing has argued, the enraged Abner was really telling Ishbaᶜal what he thought of him, for neither Saul nor Ishbaᶜal had shown *ḥesed* to him. Abner was portraying himself as master and making Ishbaᶜal as small and insignificant as possible. When the king demonstrated *ḥesed*, reciprocity was not obligatory (cf. Gen. 21:23; II Sam. 9:1, 3; 10:2; I Kings 2:7; 20:31; Ezra 7:28; 9:9; Esther 2:9, 17; Prov. 20:28; Isa. 16:5; Ps. 101:1). In II Sam. 10:2 where reciprocal action may appear to be implied, Masing argued that the *ḥesed* of Naḥash reflects a time when David was not yet king and David was somehow dependent upon his goodness. David, in offering *ḥesed* to Naḥash' son, was suggesting that the young man enter into a dependency relationship with him. Gen. 21:23 clearly indicates that Abimelech considered himself to be Abraham's vassal. By calling Israel's rulers "*ḥesed* kings" (I Kings 20:31) monarchs were reminded of their responsibility for kind action to the people, and a contrast was made between the behavior of Israel's monarchs and the despotic action of kings in other nations (cf. Prov. 20:28; Isa. 16:5).[57]

David asked Jonathan for a demonstration of *ḥesed* (I Sam. 20:8) for previously they had made a covenant before Yahweh. Later Jonathan asked David to show the *ḥesed* of Yahweh to him and his house (I Sam. 20:14 f.). Masing believed that here it was demonstrated that only the stronger can show *ḥesed* to the weaker, and that Jonathan was assuming that David would become king. David's request for *ḥesed* reveals that those bound in a covenant were committed to the exercising of *ḥesed* to the weaker party in the contract. Rahab stood in a similar relationship to the spies (Josh. 2:12–14), for Rahab in a given moment could show *ḥesed* to the men, but she knew that later they would be in a position to show her *ḥesed*. The reasons behind the reciprocal aspects are obvious for both counted upon a change occurring in the situation, and Rahab bound the men by oath to perform *ḥesed*.[58]

The only place where it can be assumed that a commoner showed *ḥesed* to a monarch is in II Sam. 16:17, but, Masing has pointed out, David was no longer monarch, but a commoner, as was his friend Ḥushai. Reciprocal *ḥesed* may have existed among friends (cf. Job 6:14). A host might demonstrate *ḥesed* to his guests and expect the

[57] *Ibid.*, p. 48. [58] *Ibid.*, p. 49.

return of *ḥesed* when he visited them. The situation in which Lot requested *ḥesed* of his guests is not normal for Lot perceived that they were not human (Gen. 19:19).

Masing rejected Glueck's thesis that sons were obligated to show *ḥesed* to their fathers, and stated that although fathers might show *ḥesed* to their children, children did not show *ḥesed* to their fathers. The only exception is found in Gen. 47:29 in which Joseph stood high over his father Jacob, and Jacob recognized this difference in status.

Only in Gen. 20:13 is a woman said to have shown *ḥesed* to a man. In this instance Abraham was unimportant as he was only the companion of a rich and beautiful woman. References in Jer. 2:2, Ruth 3:10 and perhaps Hos. 6:4 may designate the *ḥesed* a bride gave to the bridegroom, but interpretation of these passages must remain uncertain because of lack of information about how Israelite maidens thought in this matter, although perhaps there is implied a giving away of oneself.

A master or mistress might show *ḥesed* to a servant, and a rich and powerful individual could demonstrate *ḥesed* to less fortunate relatives (Gen. 24:49). The interpretation of Ruth 2:20 must remain open for it is not clear whether *ḥesed* came from Yahweh or Boaz.

Glueck has maintained that in the prophetic emphasis on *ḥesed* the community expands to become mankind, and that in prophetic and wisdom literature *ḥesed* denotes a pattern of human behavior. Masing contended that it is necessary to remember that the prophet did not speak to all mankind but to a special group, and only later was it assumed that prophetic writings were directed toward all men. Such an assumption tends to move *ḥesed* from its earlier meaning of concrete action to a way of thinking. The complaint of Hos. 4:1 is that *ḥesed ʾemeth* and *daʿath ʾelohim* are absent, and here *ḥesed* means a pattern of human behavior. It can be maintained that in *daʿath ʾelohim* both *ḥesed* and *ʾemeth* are assumed, but whether Hosea thought about this is questionable. Hosea 6:6 suggests that *ḥesed* and *daʿath ʾelohim* are part of a larger concept embracing the totality of human life. *Ḥesed* in Hosea is an attitude rather than a concrete act and perhaps "humanity," "loyalty to divine law which protects the weak" would suitably translate the sense of *ḥesed*.

In Wisdom literature with its universalistic emphasis it is never said that he who gives *ḥesed* receives it from others. Here *ḥesed* has a sense of alms or a gift and he who gives alms receives no alms from others. Because the giving of alms was pleasant to Yahweh, *ḥesed* might be rendered by "piety," *ẓedakah* by alms. During the period of critical cultural change wrought by Persian and Greek influences the two terms merged and "to do *ḥesed*" could mean a specific act, but it is preferable to translate the phrase by "to show piety through performing a socially useful deed," but here *ḥesed* implies not a single act but an attitude (Ecclus. 46:7; 49:3). Most references to *ḥesed* are to the *ḥesed* of God and usually a request is made that God might exert his *ḥesed* on the praying one. Only in rare instances is a single concrete action implied (cf. Gen. 24:12, 14, 27; II Sam. 15:20; Ruth 1:8; Ps. 85:8; 86:13; 90:14). Generally only a benevolent expression of conduct is signified, for the praying one asks only an attitude from which may come that which is pleasant. In general, it appears that in older times an individual could not receive divine *ḥesed* for himself, (excluding II Sam. 15:20), but God does demonstrate *ḥesed* to the Patriarchs (Gen. 24:12, 14, 27; 32:10; Deut. 7:12; Mic. 7:20; Ps. 98:3) and not through compulsion but by free will. The paralleling of *ḥesed* and *bᵉrit* in Deut. 7:12 does not make them almost equivalent, for he who has entered into a covenant with a weaker has already demonstrated *ḥesed* and thus *ḥesed* is already a factor in the covenant. The covenant with God provides assurance of the consistency of relationships.[59]

The concept of a Davidic covenant appears only in a few places (I Kings 8:23; II Chron. 6:14; Isa. 55:3; cf. Neh. 1:5; 9:23; Dan. 9:4), and there appears to have been a difficulty in making the idea that God made a covenant with David generally acceptable. References are generally made to the eternal *ḥesed* promised by Yahweh to the dynasty. On occasion it is suggested that for Yahweh to forsake this *ḥesed* would be tantamount to a denial of divine constancy (Ps. 89:34). The covenant of Yahweh with his people is not stressed as much as Yahweh's goodness, and often *ḥesed* appears as a parallel to *ᶜasa* or *pᵉdut* or *ᵓemet*, and Yahweh forgives the sin of the people (cf. Num. 14:19; Mic. 7:18; Lam. 3:3 ff.; Ps. 77:9; 90:14 where *raḥamim* stands as a parallel). Subsequent generations were able to participate in the covenant by which Yahweh demonstrated *ḥesed* to his people (Deut. 7:9, 12; Neh. 9:32; Mic. 7:20). When the covenant was violated Yahweh's *ḥesed* was not revoked but assumed a new emphasis of forebearance, tenderness, reconcilability. In the next development *ḥesed* became a characteristic inseparable from Yahweh and no longer meant a specific act or mode of acting, but rather that which is the basis for action. If one considered himself to be in proper covenantal relationships it was unnecessary to change the sense of *ḥesed*, but only to set narrow limits for the covenant. Thus the covenant came

[59] *Ibid.*, p. 54.

to have both wider and narrower meanings which tended to merge into one another. The inner group appealed not to the covenant but to Yahweh's *ḥesed* so that in later times the meaning of *ḥesed* was affected.

Masing traced the development of this pattern. In older literature and in literature displaying archaic motifs Yahweh's *ḥesed* is a deed and not a basis for an act. In later times the plural form *ḥasadim* was used for individual acts of God (apart from Gen. 32:11 only in late passages: Isa. 55:3; 63:7; Lam. 3:22; Ps. 17:7; 25:7; 89:2, 50; 106:7, 45; 107:43; Ecclus. 51:8). In late literature the term is used with reference to a specific class of persons associated with the temple or God and meant "pious acts" (II Chron. 32:32; 35:26; Neh. 13:14) and no reciprocal action is implied. By the time of Ben Sirach this use of the expression seems to have disappeared for he knows only the *ḥasadim* of God.

With reference to *ḥasid*, Masing noted that in Deut. 33:8 *ḥasidekha* is an infinitive and Moses is called *ʾish ḥasidekha* because he arranged a potlatch whose participants became Levites. There are places where *ḥasid* means "he who exercises *ḥesed*" (II Sam. 22:26; Ps. 18:26; 145:7; Jer. 3:12).

The term *ḥasidah* Masing explained as a feminine form of *ḥasid* and theorized that perhaps it is to be explained by flocks of storks reminding proto-Aramaean watchers of persons hurrying to a potlatch, or as the term means "she who summons to a potlatch," the holding of the potlatch may have been related to the migration of storks.

Masing realized how close he had brought *ḥesed* to *ḥen* but argued that *ḥen* was also shown to those with whom one has close ties (Gen. 30:27; 47:29; Num. 32:5; I Sam. 20:3; etc.) and in places *ḥesed* and *ḥen* occur together. Only in the older language does *ḥen* refer to God (it is only found in Ps. 45:3; 84:12 in the sense of "beauty") for *ḥesed* usurps its function and displaces it. *Ḥen*, Masing stated, never means "grace" or "favor" but rather designates a characteristic best interpreted as "beauty," "charm," "pleasantness," for *ḥen* is a prerequisite for a demonstration of *ḥesed*.

Professor Aubrey Johnson in an analysis of *ḥesed* paralleling in many respects, but making no reference to, the work of Nelson Glueck, has written that the intimate relationship existing between *berith* and *ḥesed* in the human covenants in I Sam. 20:8 ff. and II Sam. 9:1 ff. reveal that *ḥesed* connotes loyalty to covenantal terms.[60] The connec-

[60] Aubrey R. Johnson, "Hesed and Hasid," *Interpretationes ad Vetus Testamentum Pertinentes Sigmundo Mowinckel* (Oslo: Fabritius and Sønner, 1955), pp. 100–12.

tion between the words is given stronger expression in passages relating to divine-human covenants where the emphasis is upon Yahweh's loyalty to those who keep his laws as in Deut. 7:9, 12; I Kings 8:23; II Chron. 6:14; Neh. 1:5; 9:32; and Dan. 9:4. The particular expression that Yahweh will keep "*b^{e}rit* and *ḥesed*" is, Johnson notes, of Deuteronomic origin, and in this phrase "the second term may be said to sum up the content or implications of the first." Maintenance of covenant designates Yahweh as "the faithful God" (*haʾel hanneʾ^{e}man*). Further demonstration of the relationship between *b^{e}rit* and *ḥesed* is found in the form in which the covenantal promise regarding David was observed in the Jerusalem cultus as shown in Ps. 89:29–38. Here as in other passages the root *ʾmn* with its sense of faithfulness suggests "actual fidelity in personal relationships." The close relationship between *ʾ^{e}met* and *ḥesed* as in the syntax of Prov. 16:6 suggests hendiadys. A similar relationship appears to exist between *ḥesed* and *ʾ^{e}munah*, for with but a single exception (Ps. 89:25) "the order of reference is regularly that of *ḥesed* followed by *ʾ^{e}munah* so that here again the mention of *ḥesed* apparently seems to recall the root *ʾmn* in its connotation of 'faithfulness,' " further strengthening the argument that *ḥesed* has the basic significance of "loyalty."

Nevertheless, Johnson argued that the English word "loyalty" was not an adequate translation because of the close association between *ḥesed* and the root *rḥm* which relates to compassion, mercy, or sympathy, so that *ḥesed* without losing its primary meaning of "loyalty" becomes "charged with an indefinable (but quite perceptible) emotional content." The English word "devotion" Johnson suggests is a possible translation inasmuch as "*ḥesed* denotes, above all, a quality to which a man is found pledging himself on oath."

Just as *ḥesed* signifies "devotion" so the term *ḥasid* means "devotee" or in certain contexts, "one who is devout," and *ḥasid* in the masculine form is used almost exclusively of men in terms of relationships with God. Yahweh's summons in Ps. 50:5 not only brings out this meaning of *ḥasid* but demonstrates the close relationship of the term to *b^{e}rit*. On the other hand *ḥasid* through association with the root *ʾmn* in Ps. 12:2; 31:24; the root *ysr* in Ps. 97:10 f.; Prov. 2:7 f.; Mic. 7:2; the root *ẓdk* in Ps. 37:28 f.; 97:10 f.; and the root *tmm* in II Sam. 22:26; Prov. 2:7 f., etc., may have reference to characteristic qualities of the devout one, making *ḥasid* an appropriate term for usage in the Maccabaean era to designate the Jew zealously devoted to Torah (I Macc. 2:42; 7:13; II Macc. 14:6). *Ḥasid* is used to describe Yahweh in Ps. 145:17 and in Jer. 3:11 f. where the emphasis is upon the devotion of Yahweh which transcends that of his people. *Ḥesed*, therefore, connoting more than can be embraced in the legalistic terminology of the covenant can be understood in the words of W. Robertson Smith as "the virtue that knits together society."

Edmond Jacob, having acknowledged his debt to Glueck for the demonstration of the relationship between *ḥesed* and covenant, goes on to agree further that *ḥesed* has no equivalent in modern languages and that etymological studies give little aid beyond the indication that the primitive significance of the term was "strength."[61] Where *ḥesed* is used in reference to the attitudes of man toward God, Jacob suggests that the term "religion" might be employed signifying that which binds man to God, much as the Latin *pietas* described not only the attitude of the believer toward his God but also that of a son towards his father, a chief to his followers, or a God toward his believers. For human relationships *ḥesed* implies concepts of mercy, benevolence, and loyalty. God's *ḥesed* is revealed in and through the covenant, and to this permanent *ḥesed* every member of the covenant community may appeal.[62] In the Prophets, and particularly in Hosea, Jacob says the *ḥesed* concept is deepened and moves beyond the covenant in its significance. Thus violation of the covenant by the human participants does not necessarily signify the ending or withdrawing of *ḥesed*. In this context Jacob discusses Hos. 2:21; Jer. 3:12; Isa. 54:7 f.,

> In such passages *chesed* is no longer the bond upholding the covenant, it is the very source of the attitude which impels God to enter into relation with his people, therefore in reading them we must remove the strictly legal conception as N. Glueck has defined it and translate by love or grace.[63]

He argues that the terms *ḥen* and *raḥamim* replace *b^erit* in making explicit the meaning of *ḥesed* in such passages as Exod. 34:7; Num. 14:19; Isa. 63:7; Jer. 32:18; Lam. 3:32; Neh. 13:22, and Ps. 86:5; 106:7–45; 145:8. These terms do not belong to "the language of covenant and are used only in a unilateral sense which excludes reciprocity."[64] Thus *ḥesed* can be seen as such an unexpected act as to be classified as a miracle (cf. Ps. 4:4; 17:7; 31:22; 107:8, 15,

[61] Edmond Jacob, *Theologie de l'Ancien Testament* (Neuchatel: Delachaux & Niestle, 1955). English edition, *Theology of the Old Testament*, trans. by A. W. Heathcote and P. J. Allcock (New York: Harper Brothers, 1958), pp. 103 f.

[62] *Ibid.*, pp. 104–5.

[53] *Ibid*., p. 106.

[64] *Ibid.*, p. 106.

21, 31). Like Eichrodt, Jacob draws attention to the fact that with the deepening of the *ḥesed* concept there was a simultaneous "extension of its temporal significance" so that it extended into the future as well as belonging to the past, broadening its spatial characteristics to embrace all of creation (cf. Ps. 33:5; 36:7; 119:64; 136:5–9). He concludes that *ḥesed* "is particularly suitable for expressing that Yahweh was an active power in the midst of men, a power from which they could not escape."[65]

As an introduction to a discussion of the love for God in the Old Testament, Claude Wiéner briefly reviewed the various scholarly studies made of divine-human relationships, including researches into the meaning of *ḥesed*.[66] Noting the emphasis on the contractual nature of *ḥesed* first recognized by Glueck and sustained by others, Wiéner also recognized the work of Asensio with its stress on the voluntary or gratuitous love involved in *ḥesed*, as well as the work of those who have discovered a developmental or evolutionary trend in the interpretation of the word. Although Wiéner does not pursue the analysis further he suggests that the question of the precise meaning of *ḥesed* is still open and that until such meaning is determined the full comprehension of the love for God in the Old Testament is impossible.

A study of the meaning of the concepts of grace and truth in the Gospel of John led Lester J. Kuyper to suggest that in using terms so familiar from the Psalms and prophetic writings, the gospel writer was directing the reader to the Old Testament view of God.[67] The term "grace," Kuyper associated with *ḥesed*, and to elucidate the meaning drew directly on Glueck's study for examples and interpretation. Concerning the secular use of *ḥesed* Kuyper concluded that "in the performance of *ḥesed* one expects to find loyalty, mutual reciprocity, genuine faithfulness or brotherly love and affection. *Ḥesed* is not an outburst of unlooked-for mercy, nor an arbitrary demonstration of favor. It is within a covenant or fellowship or family circle that members of a fellowship demonstrate *ḥesed* by fidelity and loyalty to those in that fellowship."[68] The term "truth" (*ʾemet*) like *ḥesed*, describing an action rather than a concept, stands in a relationship of hendiadys to *ḥesed* and when they appear together they

[65] *Ibid.*, p. 107.

[66] Claude Wiéner, *Recherches sur L'amour pour Dieu dans L'Ancien Testament* (Paris: Letouzey et Ane, 1957).

[67] Lester J. Kuyper, "Grace and Truth," *Reformed Review*, Vol. 16, No. 1, (1962), pp. 1–16; "Grace and Truth," *Interpretation*, January 1964, pp. 3–19.

[68] Kuyper, "Grace and Truth," *Reformed Review*, p. 3.

convey the sense of "faithful loyalty or dependability in covenantal fellowship."[69]

Utilizing the distinction between *ḥen* and *ḥesed* drawn by Lofthouse, Kuyper wrote that "*ḥen* is a gracious unmerited favor which a superior bestows on an inferior,"[70] and *ḥesed*, also "an act of goodness" functions within "the context of a covenant or intimate fellowship."

Basic to the discussion of divine *ḥesed* is the understanding of the covenant concept which had been related through the studies of Mendenhall to contract patterns prevalent among Israel's neighbors.[71] Mendenhall distinguished between two types of covenant, the first between equals, the second between inferior and superior groups or individuals. In the latter, participation in the covenant by the superior becomes a generous act by which the superior is obligated to protect the welfare of the inferior, and wherein the inferior must perform service for the superior. This second covenant form is related to the Exodus tradition, and God's covenant with Israel becomes an act of unmerited favor or "grace" (Pauline *charis*) with the term *ḥesed* conveying the sense of God's fidelity to the nation because of the covenant. *Ḥesed* "as covenantal loyalty" Kuyper believes can be observed in the teaching of some of the prophets, as in Hos. 2:19 f., and Isa. 54:8 f.

Breach of covenant initiates need for forgiveness, and Kuyper noted that Glueck concluded from a study of Num. 14:18 that God forgives because of his *ḥen* which, Kuyper said, is an act of unqualified grace. The covenant itself rests upon unmerited favor. It is within the covenant that God has established the relationship of *ḥesed* and *ᵓemet*. When the covenant is violated the breach is healed through God's gracious compassion and the divine relationship to the community now restored to favor is *ḥesed* and *ᵓemet*.

Israel's response to divine *ḥesed* is to be found in Deut. 6:5 and in Hosea where the emphasis is upon the deep personal relationship binding God and his people, described as the loyal and faithful relationship of husband and wife, and it is *ḥesed* and justice that Israel is to maintain (Hos. 4:1; 6:4–6) — *ḥesed* expressed toward God and demonstrated among the people. Kuyper recognized that his conclusions failed to satisfy every use of *ḥesed*. In Ps. 59:9 f., 16 f.; 62:11 f.; 144:2 the sense of *ḥesed* is of "power" or "strength." In Isa. 40:6 most translators follow the LXX using *doxa* rather than *ḥasdo* as

[69] *Ibid.*, p. 4. [70] *Ibid.*, p. 5.

[71] George E. Mendenhall, *Law and Covenant in Israel and the Ancient Near East* (Pittsburgh: The Biblical Colloquium, 1955), pp. 24–50.

the basis of translation, but in view of the alternate meaning, Kuyper suggests that Isa. 40:6 might be translated "all flesh is grass and all its strength as the flower of the field," the emphasis being upon the feebleness of the flower.

Having laid this foundation Kuyper applied his findings to the Johannine gospel. In the Prologue "And the Word became flesh and dwelt among us, full of grace and truth" (John 1:14), Kuyper suggested that the terms used in the Old Testament to describe the God of Israel are employed here to attest the "full deity" of Jesus. "What was said of God in the Old Testament is here said to be equally true of Jesus of Nazareth."[72] However, the Gospel writer uses "grace" (*charis*) only four times in 1:14–17 and then drops it. Twice it is used with truth. Kuyper believes that the term "truth" which appears twenty-five times is made to carry the implication of "grace and truth." Although some passages appear to support the sense of truth (*aletheia*) as contrasted with that which is false (cf. 4:18; 6:55; 15:1), elsewhere the Hebrew concept of *ʾemet* with its stress on reliability and fidelity are implied as in 3:21; 17:17–19. In Jesus' intercessory prayer (17:17–19) "Sanctify them in the truth, thy word is truth. As thou didst send me into the world, so I have sent them into the world. And for their sakes I sanctify myself, that they may be sanctified in truth," sanctification seems to signify separation for faithful service. "Truth," embodying implications derived from the Old Testament denotes divine fidelity manifested in Jesus and communicated through him to his followers. "To be consecrated or to be sanctified through the truth, therefore, is to possess steadfast devotion by means of the steadfastness of God communicated through Jesus Christ."[73]

In Pilate's question to Jesus "What is truth" Kuyper found the convergence of *ḥen*, *ḥesed*, and *ʾemet*. Jesus, in conversation with Pilate, declares himself to be the manifestation of divine truth so that those who are of the truth obey his voice. The emphasis here, Kuyper has written, goes beyond the Greek idea of truth versus falsehood, and involves the Old Testament stress on the redemptive, gracious, faithfulness of God, suggesting that this is what is revealed in Jesus.

E. M. Good, writing in the *Interpreter's Dictionary of the Bible*[74]

[72] Kuyper, *op. cit.*, p. 11.

[73] *Ibid.*, p. 13.

[74] E. M. Good, "Love in the Old Testament," *The Interpreter's Dictionary of the Bible* (New York, Nashville: Abingdon Press, 1962), Vol. III, pp. 164–68.

finds in the use of *ḥesed* in Ruth 3:10 sexual overtones as well as the concept of loyalty. He proceeds, in his analysis, to describe *ḥesed* in terms of "kindness" and "loyalty" signifying life's most desirable quality (Prov. 19:22). *Ḥesed* may mean kindness shown to the poverty-stricken or unfortunate (Prov. 14:21, 31; 19:17; 28:8). It may refer to the loyalty of Yahweh as the end product of a human covenant (I Sam. 20:14). Because of the reciprocal nature of human covenants "to show *ḥesed*" nearly always means the return of a favor (Gen. 40:14; Josh. 2:12, 14; Judg. 1:24; 8:35).

On occasion *ḥesed* is used with reference to the election-love of Yahweh, the choice of Israel as an act of love by Yahweh (Exod. 15:13; Ps. 106:7; Neh. 9:17), although elsewhere other terms such as *ʾahav* (Deut. 4:37) or *ḥovev* (Deut. 33:3) or *ʾahavah* (Hos. 11:4) may appear. In Deut. 7:13 *ḥesed* is used with reference to "covenant love" and because of the use of the phrase *bᵉrit wᵉḥesed* and the paralleling of *ḥesed* with *bᵉrit*, *ḥesed* is primarily concerned with covenant-love — a faithful, steadfast, lasting relationship. The endurance of covenant-love has, Good believes, eschatological overtones, as expressed in the formula used in relation to the Exodus tradition "for his *ḥesed* endures forever" (Ps. 136. See also I Chron. 16:34, 41; II Chron. 5:13; 7:3, 6; 20:21; Ezra 3:11; Ps. 100:5; etc.). The moral implications in the term *ḥesed* are demonstrated in Hos. 6:6; Mic. 6:8, where it is said that Yahweh prefers *ḥesed* to ritual. Good notes that in most of the Bible *ḥesed* symbolizes God's love for man and *ʾahavah* man's love for God, but Hosea reverses this pattern by expressing Yahweh's love as *ʾahavah* and human reciprocal love as *ḥesed*.

Despite research done on *ḥesed* by others subsequent to the first publication of Nelson Glueck's monograph, there can be no doubt that Glueck's interpretation has remained primary. Not only has his study been utilized by numerous scholars, but through references in the writings of others his ideas have gained wide acceptance. It is possible that the summarizing of some of the key studies of *ḥesed* may exercise a softening influence on Glueck's interpretation, and perhaps suggest that we are approaching a time when a new investigation of this important term and its relationship to words with which it is often associated including *ḥen*, *ʾemeth*, *bᵉrit*, *raḥamim*, *ʾahavah*, *ẓadik* and *ẓadikah*, etc., will have to be made. Until the time when such research is undertaken Nelson Glueck's word study will continue its important role of providing the basic interpretation of *ḥesed*.

ḤESED IN THE BIBLE

CHAPTER I

Ḥesed as Human Conduct — Its Secular Meaning

I. A PRELIMINARY CLARIFICATION OF THE CONCEPT — THOSE WHO PRACTICE ḤESED

To clarify the conceptual meaning of the word in its secular sense in the Hebrew Bible, we need first determine the persons to whom the expression refers. Proceeding from the actual usage of the word we shall fix, to the extent possible, its real and implied meaning.

A. The Ḥesed-Relationship Between Relatives and Related Tribes

In Gen. 47:29 (J^1)[1] Jacob, about to die, asks his son Joseph, to swear to him that he will show him חסד ואמת. Abraham asks his wife, Sarah, to render *ḥesed* to him, Gen. 20:13 (E^2). Boaz praises Ruth, Ruth 3:10, for the *ḥesed* she is showing her husband and his family. Naomi, Ruth 2:20, blesses her kinsman, Boaz, for having shown *ḥesed* to Ruth.[2] Abraham's servant, Gen 24:49 (J^1), asks the family of Nahor, Abraham's brother,[3] whether they are willing to show חסד ואמת to his master. Saul, I Sam. 15:6 (S^b) recalls the *ḥesed* which the friendly and related Kenites[4] had demonstrated toward the Israelites when they went up from Egypt.

[1] In the differentiation of sources I mainly followed Steuernagel, *Lehrbuch der Einleitung in das Alte Testament* (Tübingen, 1912).

[2] Cf. Ch. I, pp. 40 f.

[3] Cf. Gen. 24:15, 47, 48.

[4] Cf. Judg. 4:11; 1:16; 5:24; Num. 10:29 f.

B. Between Host and Guest

The men whom Lot receives as his guests, Gen. 19:19 (J[1]), show him *ḥesed*. Raḥab renders *ḥesed* to the spies who found refuge in her house, Josh. 2:12, 14 (E[2]), and they swear to do *ḥesed* to her and her family. Abimelech asks Abraham to vow to show him the same *ḥesed* which he had displayed to Abraham, Gen. 21:23 (E[2]), in permitting him to sojourn in his land.

C. Between Allies and Their Relatives

David, reminding Jonathan of the Yahweh-covenant between them, I Sam. 20:8 (S[b]), entreats Jonathan to show him *ḥesed*. Jonathan implores David, I Sam. 20:14, 15 (S[b]), to practice forever toward him and his house the *ḥesed* which had been sworn to him in the name of Yahweh. In II Sam. 9:1, 3, 7 (Je) David shows *ḥesed* to Jonathan's son.[5]

D. Between Friends

Absalom, II Sam. 16:17 (Je), asks Ḥushai whether, in his relationship to David, Ḥushai had shown his friend *ḥesed*. David wishes to reciprocate to Ḥanun, the son of his friend Naḥash, II Sam. 10:2 (Je),[6] the same *ḥesed* that Naḥash had evinced toward him.

E. Between Ruler and Subject

Abner, II Sam. 3:8 (S[a]), speaks of the *ḥesed* he had shown to King Saul and his son Eshbaal. In II Chron. 24:22 we read that King Joash, unmindful of the *ḥesed* shown to him by his High Priest Jehoiada, caused the latter's son to be slain. Because the officers of Benhadad, defeated by Aḥab, I Kings 20:31 f.,[7] know of the reputation of the kings of Israel as being מלכי חסד, they approach Aḥab with the request to spare their king, whom they call Aḥab's servant.

[5] We may assume that the historian in Je knew of the ברית יהוה between David and Jonathan, cf. Ch. I, pp. 48 ff.

[6] I Chron. 19:2.

[7] Staerk, *Die Entstehung des Alten Testamentes.* (Berlin and Leipzig, 1918), p. 166, assigns I Kings 20 to the end of the 9th century. Cf. Steuernagel, pp. 362, 3; Kamphausen in Kautzsch's Bible[3], *et al.*

Esther 2:9, 17 speaks of the *ḥesed* which Esther had obtained from King Aḥasuerus.

F. *Ḥesed* as Merited Obligation

In Judg. 1:24 (J) we read that the spies scouting Bethel promise to show *ḥesed* to a man whom they saw leaving the city if he would indicate to them a way of entering the city. David commands Solomon to show *ḥesed* forever to the members of the house of Barzillai, I Kings 2:7 (Je), because the latter had given him aid when he fled from Absalom.[8] David, II Sam. 2:5 (S^a), blesses the men of Jabesh-gilead for having shown *ḥesed* to Saul, their deliverer. Judg. 8:35 (Rd) relates that the people of Israel did not show *ḥesed* to Gideon's family, although Gideon had been a great benefactor to the people of Israel. Joseph implores the chief butler, whose dream he had interpreted propitiously, Gen. 40:14 (E^2), to remember him and show him *ḥesed* after his reinstatement to rank and office.

Summary

From the preceding analysis it becomes clear that *ḥesed* is received or shown only by those among whom a definite relationship exists. Accordingly, what we call the *ḥesed*-relationship exists between:

A. Relatives by blood or marriage, related clans and related tribes
B. Host and guest
C. Allies and their relatives
D. Friends
E. Ruler and subject
F. Those who have gained merit by rendering aid, and the parties thereby put under obligation.

The above indicates that *ḥesed* exists between people who are in some close relationship to one another. Our next concern is to explain what *ḥesed* is. We must now deal with the extent to which the meaning of the word is influenced by the fact that *ḥesed* can be practiced only between persons who share an ethically binding relationship. The analysis of the conceptual content of the word *ḥesed* will be based on a further examination of those passages in which the word occurs in a purely secular sense.

[8] Cf. II Sam. 17:27–29; 19:32–41.

II. *ḤESED* AS CONDUCT CORRESPONDING TO A MUTUAL RELATIONSHIP OF RIGHTS AND DUTIES

A. *Ḥesed* as the Mutual Relationship of Rights and Duties Between the Members of a Family or Tribe

In ancient Israel, as well as in ancient Arabia,[9] a mutual relationship of rights and duties existed among the members of a family or among those who believed themselves to be of similar tribal ancestry. The family and tribal bonds were of primary importance.[10] The members of a family or a clan were totally dependent upon one another. They lived in a relatively closed circle, the confines of which could be widened only by the undertaking of relationships based on rights and duties assumed on a different basis. We shall treat this point later in greater detail. Such members enjoyed common rights and they had to fulfill mutual obligations. Their whole existence was governed by this concept of reciprocity. In reference to I Sam. 20:8, W. R. Smith[11] says:

> In primitive society, where every stranger is an enemy, the whole conception of the duties of humanity is framed within the narrow circle of the family or the tribe; relations of love are either identical with those of kinship or are conceived as resting on a covenant.

In ancient Israel it appears that conduct based on relationships involving rights and duties of a family or a tribal community was called *ḥesed.* We have noted [12] that only those who stood in a relationship of rights and duties to one another received and practiced *ḥesed.*

[9] The same is true of present-day Arabia as well. Cf. W. R. Smith, *Kinship and Marriage in Early Arabia* (Cambridge, 1885), pp. 22–26, 35, 56, 57, 160, 161. Pedersen, *Der Eid bei den Semiten* (Strassburg, 1914), pp. 21–23, 28, 31, 222.

[10] Benzinger, *Hebräische Archäologie* (Tübingen, 1907), pp. 102 f. "In no nation is the significance of the family as the foundation of the entire social order as clearly recognizable as in Israel . . . We get to know the Israelites still on the lowest level of political organization, at the time of clans or tribal organization, in which the family is of the utmost importance."

Cf. Nowack, *Lehrbuch der Hebräischen Archäologie* (Freiburg i.B. und Leipzig, 1894), p. 152, *et al.*

[11] *The Prophets of Israel* (Edinburgh, 1882), p. 161.

[12] *Supra*, p. 37.

This is borne out by the interpretation of *ḥesed* as mutuality or reciprocal conduct (gemeinschaftgemässen Verhaltungsweise).

I. KINSHIP

a. *Consanguinity: Father and Son*

Jacob, near death, called his son, Joseph, to ask a great favor of him, Gen. 47:29. He said, "If I have found favor[13] in your sight, put your hand under my thigh,[14] that you will show me חסד ואמת; and not bury me in Egypt." Jacob adjured Joseph to show him faithful love even after his death, and to bury him with his fathers in Canaan. Great importance was attached to burial.[15] He saw, however, the great difficulties connected with the fulfillment of his heart's desire and knew that in the natural course of events he would be buried in Egypt. For this reason he found it necessary to make his son take an oath. Joseph took this oath, and when the time came he fulfilled it.[16] Actually, no special oath should have been necessary. Had Joseph not shown faithful love to his father before his death, he would have been an unnatural son. Every son owed his father love commensurate with the demands of loyalty. Such love was based not only on personal affection but also on duty. It was the only possible conduct of a son toward his father, since they are both of the same flesh and blood.

b. *Relationship by Marriage*

(1) *Husband and wife*

When Abraham travelled to strange lands with his wife, Sarah, Gen. 20:13, he asked her during the course of their journey to pass him off as her brother, since he was afraid of being murdered because of his attractive wife. Before asking that favor of her, he reminded her of her duties toward him, saying, "This is your *ḥesed*, which you must show me: wherever we go, say that I am your brother."

[13] אם מצאתי חן בעיניך means here "If you really care for me" and is actually a term of entreaty and cannot be explained by reference to Joseph's exalted position, as Procksch says in *Die Genesis*$^{2.3}$ (Leipzig, 1924). It merely emphasizes the close relationship between father and son. He who has found חן in the eyes of another may also be shown *ḥesed*. Cf. Gen. 19:19.

[14] Gen. 24:2.

[15] Cf. Gen. 23; 50:1–11; II Sam. 2:5.

[16] Gen. 50:1–11.

There were certain fixed rules of conduct for members of a family based on reciprocity, called *ḥesed*, which obligated all members of a family to assist one another. *Ḥesed* characterized the relationship between husband and wife, and both had to comport themselves accordingly. *Ḥesed* was not merely love dependent solely on the subject but was, at the same time, loyalty and duty. Where *ḥesed* is used alone and not in the combination חסד ואמת, as is frequently the case, one may still picture mentally אמת next to חסד. Abraham, who believed his life to be in danger, could plead with Sarah to remember her *ḥesed* obligation to him and to save him by stating that she was his sister (which, in fact, she was).[17] By doing so, however, she risked the danger of having strangers expropriate her.

(2) *The redeemer and the widow of his kinsman*

Only in the Book of Ruth is the word *ḥesed* used in a sense similar to that employed in the older sources. In Ruth 3:10 it is clearly shown that *ḥesed* is that mode of conduct which is in accordance with familial obligations. Ruth obeyed her mother-in-law and hid herself close to where Boaz slept. After he had fallen asleep, she nestled at his feet. Boaz awakened at midnight and was startled to find her there. Upon his questioning, Ruth told him who she was and asked him, as a kinsman of her husband, to fulfill his obligation to her as redeemer (גאל) and to marry her. Boaz declared his willingness to do so, provided that a nearer kinsman of her husband would renounce his duties and rights. He blessed Ruth, who had so loyally shown *ḥesed* to her husband, saying, "May you be blessed by Yahweh, my daughter; you have made this last *ḥesed* greater than the first, in that you have not gone after young men, whether poor or rich." The *ḥesed* which Ruth had demonstrated to her husband even after his death, by leaving her native land and father's house and following Naomi,[18] was surpassed by the sense of love and loyalty she subsequently demonstrated. Instead of marrying a younger man, Ruth preferred to turn to the older Boaz, her husband's kinsman, in order, by virtue of this marriage, to have offspring for her husband who had died childless. Here *ḥesed* indicates a development beyond the ordinary use of the term in the older sources, since *ḥesed* in this context refers more to a subjective mode of conduct willed by an individual, and not simply

[17] Vs. 12.

[18] Cf. Nowack, *Richter, Ruth and Bücher Samuelis* (Göttingen, 1902); Bertheau, *Das Buch der Richter und Ruth* (Leipzig, 1883).

to an attitude of obligation. Ruth was by no means obliged to go with Naomi. She was as free as Naomi's other daughter-in-law to return to her own people. Yet, in faithful love she followed her mother-in-law. In true religiosity she complied with Jewish custom. Ruth took it upon herself to practice *ḥesed* in order to fulfill the obligations of a Jewish widow.

The meaning of *ḥesed* as conduct in accord with familial obligations is confirmed also in Ruth 2:20, if we understand אשר לא־עזב חסדו את־החיים ואת־המתים to refer to Boaz and not to Yahweh. In II Sam. 2:5 we have almost an exact parallel to Ruth 2:20. David blessed the men of Jabesh-gilead because they had buried Saul, saying: ברוכים אתם ליהוה אשר עשיתם החסד הזה. Boaz is blessed by Naomi, Ruth 2:20, for the kindness he had shown Ruth. She says:

ברוך הוא[19] ליהוה אשר לא־עזב חסדו את־החיים ואת־המתים.

If we accept the commonly held view according to which אשר לא־עזב is in apposition to ליהוה, this would be the only place in the Hebrew Bible where the *ḥesed* of God is mentioned in reference to the dead. The relationship between God and man, very frequently expressed by *ḥesed*, requires of man the fulfillment of certain conditions. Only those who serve God in faithfulness participate in communion with him and receive *ḥesed*[20] from him. It is very doubtful whether the dead, who in the Hebrew Bible generally are described as having absolutely no relationship with God,[21] can appear here as receiving *ḥesed* from God. The passage beginning with אשר לא־עזב is to be understood as referring to Boaz. It was he who had shown *ḥesed* to the living and the dead.[22] From his servants, Boaz discovered who Ruth was[23] and then had shown her special kindness. Further, Boaz was in no way perplexed when Ruth asked him to fulfill his obligation as "redeemer" and to marry her. She gave him no other explanation than that he was the "redeemer." Boaz was aware of his relationship to Ruth and also knew who was still a closer kinsman to her than

[19] S reads יהוה for ליהוה, cf. Kittel, *Biblia Hebraica*. This is not necessary since the above suggested meaning concludes the same.

[20] Cf. Deut. 5:10; Exod. 20:6; Deut. 7:9; II Chron. 6:14; I Kings 8:23; Dan. 9:24; Neh. 1:5; Ps. 103:17, 18; 37:28; 96:10; 86:2; I Sam. 2:9; Ps. 147:11; 119:124; 143:12; *passim*.

[21] Cf. Isaiah 38:18; Ps. 6:6; 16:10; 88:12.

[22] Ruth 1:8 also mentions conduct toward the living and the dead. Naomi blessed her daughters-in-law, saying: "May the Lord deal kindly with you, as you have dealt with the dead and with me."

[23] Ruth 2:6, 11.

he. Boaz thereupon declared, without hesitation, his readiness to marry her if the other kinsman would forego his claim.[24] His conduct toward Ruth, therefore, was in accordance with *ḥesed*. That evening, when Ruth told her mother-in-law that she had met Boaz and told her of his friendliness toward her, Naomi acknowledged him as a relative. In his conduct toward Ruth, she recognized the attitude of a relative conscious of familial obligations. By his kindness to Ruth, Boaz had honored his deceased kinsman and fulfilled his obligations, and for that Naomi blessed him.

2. THE TRIBAL COMMUNITY

a. *The Tribal Community in its More Limited Sense: Related Families*

In returning to the older sources, such as Gen. 24:49, we find that *ḥesed* means to be in accord with family obligations. Abraham's servant wanted to bring Rebecca to Abraham out of the house of Naḥor, Abraham's brother,[25] so that she might become Isaac's wife. He asked the members of her family if they were ready to show his master steadfast love, i. e., to act in accordance with their obligations as relatives of Abraham. The proof of this would be their consent to the marriage.

b. *The Tribal Community in a Broader Sense: Related Tribes*

Ḥesed, as a mode of conduct between related and friendly tribes, occurs in I Sam. 15:6. The Kenites, Israel's neighbors and close friends who were related to the Israelites through Moses' marriage,[26] had shown *ḥesed* to the Israelites in their Exodus from Egypt.[27] They had maintained that relationship toward Israel which ought to exist between relatives and friends. The Kenites, who had conducted themselves as friends[28] and relatives of Israel in time of need by performing *ḥesed* and fulfilling their mutually obligatory duties in friendly kinship, rendered loyal assistance to Israel. This *ḥesed* was later reciprocated. Saul spared them in his campaign against the

[24] Ruth 3:9 f.

[25] Cf. *supra*, fn. 3.

[26] Cf. Judges 1:16; 4:11. Kittel, *Geschichte des Volkes Israel* (Stuttgart, [6]1923), Vol. 1, pp. 318, 347 bottom; Vol. 2, p. 17; Stade, *Geschichte des Volkes Israel* (Berlin, 1887), I.1, pp. 131 f.; Budde, *Die Religion des Volkes Israel bis zur Verbannung* (Giessen, 1900), pp. 15 f.

[27] Cf. Kittel, *loc. cit.*; Stade, *loc. cit.*; cf. *supra*, fn. 4.

[28] Cf. Ch. I, pp. 49 f.

Amalekites, in whose midst they lived. The Israelites were obligated to behave toward the Kenites as the latter had conducted themselves toward the Israelites.

B. Ḥesed as the Mutual Relationship of Rights and Duties Between Host and Guest

In ancient Israel, as was the case in ancient Arabia (and also in present-day Arabia),[29] the law of hospitality was sacred. The host, if necessary, had to risk his life for his guest.[30] Host and guest stood in a reciprocal protective relationship to one another. Between them there was a relationship of rights and duties[31] comparable to that which existed between blood relatives. Host and guest became "brothers"[32] in every respect. Whoever slept in the tent of another and ate of his bread was accounted as a member of the host's family.[33] In ancient Israel, this mutual relationship of rights and duties between host and guest was called *ḥesed.*

I. Host and Guest

From Gen. 19:19 we can see how important the law of hospitality and its duties were to the ancient Israelites. Lot received in his house the three strangers (angels) who had appeared in Sodom. When the men of the city demanded that the strangers be handed over, Lot offered to bring out his chaste daughters in their place to be dealt with as they pleased. He would not, however, surrender his guests under any circumstances. He had taken them in and it was a sacred duty for him, as host, to protect them. Lot told the men of the city,[34] "But these men you may not harm, for they have come under the shelter of my roof." Angered by his refusal, they attacked Lot. He would have fared badly if his guests had not pulled him into the house and barred the door, while they afflicted the people in front with blindness. Thereupon, the strangers announced to Lot the

[29] W. R. Smith, *Kinship*, pp. 14, 41; Doughty, *Wanderings in Arabia* (London, 1908), Vol. I, p. 252; Vol. II, pp. 154, 164, 276, 277, 280.

[30] Smith, *op. cit.*, p. 41. "It is a principle alike in old and new Arabia that the guest is inviolable." Cf. Gen. 19.

[31] Pedersen, *op. cit.*, p. 25.

[32] Smith, *op. cit.*, p. 14. "A man whom one is bound to protect is . . . a brother by virtue of this bond."

[33] Cf. *supra*, fns. 29, 31.

[34] Vs. 8.

destruction of Sodom and urged him to save himself and his family by having them take refuge in the mountains.

Lot counted their aid as well as their rescuing him as *ḥesed.* He asked their permission to flee instead to a small town nearby. Lot said to one of the angels,[35] "Behold your servant has found favor in your sight since the *ḥesed* that you have shown me was great in saving my life." Because he remained faithful to his guests, he showed himself worthy to receive *ḥesed.* Under any circumstances, he had chosen to grant his guests the protection of his house and thereby put them under an obligation to be loyal to him, to render assistance and to show him *ḥesed.* Since Lot's guests are represented as angels, their *ḥesed*, their reciprocity of Lot's conduct toward them is called "great"; that is, it is portrayed as grace or mercy. In actuality, however, their *ḥesed* emanated from the mutual relationship of rights and duties between host and guest. As a true host, Lot was ready to sacrifice everything for his guests. As loyal guests, they came to his assistance. The mutuality of their relationship was determined by *ḥesed.*

Ḥesed is also to be considered as conduct emanating from the mutual relationship of rights and duties between host and guest in Josh. 2:12, 14. Joshua's spies, who lodged at Raḥab's house, were hidden by her when the King of Jericho's messengers demanded their surrender. With her assistance, the spies were able to flee and save themselves. By assisting them and by fulfilling the obligations of hospitality, Raḥab showed *ḥesed* and was true to the code governing the relationship between host and guest. Because of this, she was entitled to make them vow to show *ḥesed* to her and her family when they would return with the Israelite armies. " 'Now then, swear to me by Yahweh,' she said, 'that you also will keep faith with my father's house as I have kept faith with you.' "[36] The men took the oath and said to her, "Our life for yours;[37] if Yahweh gives us the land we will deal dutifully and loyally with you." And this oath they kept.[38]

[35] Procksch, *loc. cit.* "Thus J in the course of the conversation makes a transition to the singular, as Lot naturally addresses one particular person." Cf. also König, *Die Genesis* (Gütersloh², 1925), *loc. cit.*

[36] With Steuernagel, *Deuteronomium und Josua*² (Göttingen, 1923), and Gressmann, *Die Anfänge Israels*² (Göttingen, 1922), regarding this passage, ונתתם לי אות אמת is to be omitted.

[37] In accordance with Steuernagel, *loc. cit.*, and Gressmann, *loc. cit.*, אם לא תגידו את דברנו זה is to be omitted. The spies had no right to impose another condition on Raḥab. She had shown them *ḥesed* and they were obligated to reciprocate with *ḥesed.* Gressmann omits also נפשינו תחתיכם למות.

[38] Josh. 6:22, 23.

2. THE *GER* AND HIS PROTECTOR

Gen. 21:23 also belongs to the category of *ḥesed* as the proper conduct in the relationship between host and guest, for such qualities as reciprocity, obligation and loyalty appear distinctively as characteristics of *ḥesed*. Abraham had been received hospitably in Gerar, as a *ger*. He had put himself under the protection of Abimelech, King of Gerar,[39] thereby creating a mutual relationship of rights and duties corresponding to *ḥesed*. The *ger* had certain obligations to his protector[40] and vice versa. For this reason, Abimelech returned Sarah to Abraham when he learned that she was the latter's wife. A protector could not take away the wife of a *ger* since that would have been a rupture of the mutual relationship existing between them. Because of Abimelech's integrity, the bond between Abraham and Abimelech was strengthened. By doing *ḥesed*, he could, on his part, adjure Abraham to remain loyal and to show *ḥesed* toward him and his house forever.[41] Abimelech said to Abraham: "Now therefore swear unto me here by God that you will not deal falsely with me or with my offspring or with my posterity, but as I have dealt loyally with you, you will deal with me and with the land where you have sojourned as a stranger."[42] Abimelech explicitly referred to Abraham as a *ger*. It is shown here that חסד, which appears as the opposite of שקר, shows חסד as conduct in accordance with the demands of loyalty which contains the concept of אמת or אמונה.[43] Abraham swore the oath,[44] and on the basis of the חסד shown by the one and sworn to by the other, Abraham and Abimelech made a covenant.[45] Here, and as we shall see further in I Sam. 20:8,[46] it is obvious that *ḥesed* represents the real essence of the covenant.[47] By *ḥesed* one must understand in this context the attitude stemming from the mutual relationship of rights and duties between protector and *ger*.[48]

[39] Gunkel (*Die Urgeschichte und die Patriarchen*² [Göttingen, 1921]) translates אשר גרתה בה with "where you have sought protection."

[40] Cf. I Sam. 27:12, 28:1 f.; W. R. Smith, *op. cit.*, pp. 42 f., points to the mutual relationship of rights and duties between patron and *ger* in Arab countries.

[41] The details in this verse are almost entirely identical with those in Josh. 2:12. There we likewise find hospitality, the granting of *ḥesed*, and the demand for, and taking of, an oath in reciprocation of *ḥesed*.

[42] König, *loc. cit.*, translates *ḥesed* as "loyalty."

[43] Cf. Ps. 89:34, וחסדי לא אפיר [L. אסיר] מעמו ולא אשקר באמונתו.

[44] Vs. 24. [45] Vs. 32.

[46] Ch. I, pp. 46 ff.

[47] *Ibid.*; Ps. 25:10; 103:17, 18.

[48] Prof. Stärk pointed to the Levites as God's *gerim* in a seminar session in the

C. Ḥesed as the Mutual Relationship of Rights and Duties Between Allies

In ancient Israel no mutual relationship of rights and duties was considered of greater importance than that between allies.[49] Between the members of an alliance, just as between blood relatives, *ḥesed* was the only possible mode of conduct. Whoever did not act in accordance with *ḥesed* was expelled from the alliance as from the family. Whoever did not fulfill his duties in such a community forfeited his right to protection and assistance which, in effect, was virtually a death sentence. Allies had the same rights and obligations as those who were blood relations. Allies, for all practical purposes, were אחים, "brothers." In Amos 1:9, for example, a covenant is mentioned which is called "the brotherly covenant" (ברית אחים), which made brothers of the allies.[50] This passage could almost be translated: "They did not think of their brotherly obligations."[51]

In I Sam. 20:8 *ḥesed* appears quite clearly as conduct in accordance with the mutual relationship of rights and duties between allies. Between David and Jonathan, who were already united by the bonds of friendship (which, as we shall see, also required the *ḥesed* relationship), there existed a sacred covenant concluded in the name of Yahweh.[52] Through this covenant their friendship was transformed into brotherhood and *ḥesed* was the mode of conduct each had to assume toward the other. The *bᵉrith* they entered[53] "put both under the solemn obligation to take care of the welfare and safety of his friend. David, therefore, appeals to this obligation when asking for Jonathan's protection. Any breach of this obligation was called עון and was punishable by death."[54] David implored Jonathan to protect

---

summer semester of 1925. *Ḥesed* also existed between Yahweh as the protector and his *gerim*, the Levites, who had no part in any secular communal life but depended entirely on Yahweh and his service. Cf. Deut. 33:8, 9. איש חסידך are the "men of your faithful one" (probably Moses, as in König, *Das Deuteronomium* [Leipzig, 1917]; Prof. Stärk in seminar sessions). To the איש חסידך belongs the man who by loyalty to God wins acceptance into his community.

49 W. R. Smith, *The Prophets of Israel*, p. 161.

50 W. R. Smith, *Kinship*, p. 14: "Brotherhood in the semitic tongues is a very loose word; even covenant relations may make men brothers." Cf. Pedersen, *op. cit.*, pp. 33, 222.

51 Thus in Kraetzschmar, *Die Bundesvorstellung im Alten Testament* (Marburg, 1896), p. 22.

52 Cf. I Sam. 18:3; II Sam. 21:7.

53 Doughty, *op. cit.*, Vol. I, p. 244.

54 Kraetzschmar, *op. cit.*, p. 20.

him against Saul, the latter's father, since he feared for his life. In doing so, he pointed to the covenant between them. He asked for *ḥesed*, conduct in accord with the relationship existing between him and Jonathan. It was Jonathan's duty, required by *ḥesed*, to come to David's assistance and, if necessary, to sacrifice his own life for that of his friend. David said: "You should show your servant brotherliness, for you have brought your servant into a Yahweh-Covenant with you."

It could hardly be stated more explicitly that *ḥesed* is the conduct required in the mutual relationship between allies. The obligations and rights acquired through a covenant are translated into corresponding actions through *ḥesed*. *Ḥesed* is the real essence of *berith*, and it can almost be said that it is its very content. The possibility of the origin and existence of a covenant was based on the existence of *ḥesed*. Where חסד and ברית occur side by side in the Bible, they are not to be understood as being entirely synonymous but as being mutually contingent upon one another.[55] In those passages where חסד and ברית seem parallel to each other, everyday usage may not have made a sharp distinction. To this extent, Elbogen is probably right in his assumption that חסד has the same meaning as ברית or שבועה.[56]

Ḥesed is also used in I Sam. 20:14, 15, to signify the attitude which must exist between allies. The text is mutilated but the meaning is clear.[57] David, who had implored Jonathan to grant him *ḥesed* as he had promised, was in turn entreated by Jonathan never to withhold from him and his house the *ḥesed* of the covenant sworn to him in the name of Yahweh. Jonathan asked David to keep faith with him

[55] Cf. Deut. 7:9, 12; I Kings 8:23; II Chron. 6:14; Dan. 9:4; Neh. 1:5; 19:32; Ps. 89:29; 106:45; 50:5; 25:10; 103:17, 18; Isa. 54:10; 55:3.

[56] Elbogen, "חסד = obligation, promise, confirmation," in "Festschrift für Paul Haupt," 1926. Referring to I Sam. 20:15, the only passage treated by him, where *ḥesed* is used in a secular sense: "Perhaps חסד in I Sam. 20:15 is also to be understood in the sense of a covenant in which case it would be connected with תכרית in a sense opposite to that of כרת as used elsewhere."

[57] H. P. Smith, *A Critical and Exegetical Commentary on the Books of Samuel* (Edinburgh, 1904), verse 14 reads:

וְלֹא (אִם) עודני חי וְלֹא תעשה
עמדי חסד
וְלֹא אמות ולא תכרית את חסדך מעם
ביתי עד עולם

Cf. Budde, *Die Bücher Samuel* (Tübingen und Leipzig, 1902). Nowack, *loc. cit.*, and Wellhausen, *Der Text der Bücher Samuelis* (Göttingen, 1871).

and never to reject him. Jonathan implored David not to have him and his family slain as a possible threat to the throne, according to Oriental practice, when he was king and no longer had anything to fear from his enemies.[58] In the latter case, he called on Yahweh to demand this of David.[59] The *ḥesed* to which Jonathan appealed was the *ḥesed* sworn to in the name of Yahweh, as in vs. 8; חסד יהוה and the חסד which emanates from a ברית יהוה are identical. In vs. 15 the *ḥesed* which Jonathan asked from David for himself and his house is naturally the same *ḥesed* as in vs. 14. David was obligated to show Jonathan and his family, during Jonathan's lifetime and beyond, the brotherliness he had sworn to him.[60] The concept of duty is very closely related to *ḥesed*, especially as duty was commonly understood in ancient Israel. Duty was but another facet of right.[61] *Ḥesed* was the relationship among people who formed a fellowship which required the fulfillment of mutual responsibilities.

After becoming king, II Sam. 9:1, 3, 7, David intended to show *ḥesed*, for Jonathan's sake, toward Saul's house, which had been almost entirely exterminated. He recalled his relationship to Jonathan and was ready to offer Jonathan's family the *ḥesed* which he owed to him and his house. The loyal love, which David practiced when he learned of Meribaal's existence, by restoring to him his grandfather's possessions and assigning him a seat at his own table, was in reciprocity for the *ḥesed* shown him by Jonathan. Although II Sam. 9:1, 3, 7, belongs to Je, an older source[62] than I Sam. 20:8, 14, 15, which Steuernagel[63] attributed to S^b, *ḥesed* has certainly the same

[58] Cf. I Sam. 24:22; I Kings 15:29; 16:11; II Kings 10:6; 11:1.

[59] Smith, *loc. cit.*, vss. 15, 16 read:

וְלֹא בהכרית
יהוה איבי דוד מעל פני האדמה וְיִכָּרֵת (בית)
יהונתן עם בית שאול ובקש יהוה מיד דוד

Cf. Nowack, *loc. cit.*

[60] Budde, *loc. cit.*, and Driver, *Notes on the Hebrew Text of the Books of Samuel* (Oxford, 1890), want to read חסד אלהים for חסד יהוה as in II Sam. 9:3. If a change is to be made at all, II Sam. 9:3 should be changed to read חסד יהוה. Reuss, *Das Alte Testament* (Braunschweig, 1892), grasped the proper sense in translating חסד יהוה as "the friendship sworn to before Yahweh." Kittel's translation "mercy" (in Yahweh's manner) is not possible (in Kautzsch, *Die Heilige Schrift* [Tübingen, 1922]).

[61] "Concepts like obligation and right are unilateral in our thinking since we start with the individual. The Semite proceeds from the communal. 'Obligation' for him is part of a larger concept which also includes 'right'; and this broader concept is the relationship between persons who belong together." Pedersen, *op. cit.*, p. 9.

[62] Steuernagel, *Introduction*, p. 335.

[63] Steuernagel, *ibid.*, p. 319.

meaning in both. Nothing speaks against the assumption that Je also knew of the ברית יהוה and the חסד יהוה connected with it. It may be assumed that Je regarded the *ḥesed* which David intended to show to the remnant of Saul's house, as stemming not from friendship alone but also from the sacred covenant in accordance with the obligation incurred by invoking Yahweh's name. This was the view of the narrator in Je,[64] who wrote in II Sam. 21:7: "But the king spared Mephibosheth, the son of Saul's son Jonathan, because of the Yahweh-Oath which was between David and Jonathan the son of Saul." The *ḥesed* shown by David to Jonathan's house was neither grace nor mercy; it was brotherliness required by covenantal loyalty.

One would like to read in vs. 3, as in I Sam. 20:14, חסד יהוה instead of חסד אלהים, which would better fit the context. H. P. Smith,[65] however, holds that חסד אלהים means the same as חסד יהוה. He says: "It is difficult to suppose the meaning to be 'kindness such as God shows.' More probably it is the kindness imposed by God in obligation of the oath." This interpretation is possible, perhaps, if one considers Gen. 21:23, where Abimelech asks Abraham to swear to him in the name of אלהים, to keep faith with him and show him חסד. If the word אלהים is to be kept here, it can well mean that David was ready to show the same inviolable *ḥesed* as does God to those who are near to him, for the zeal for duty and the inviolability of an oath are characteristic of *ḥesed*.

D. *Ḥesed* as Conduct Stemming From the Mutual Relationship of Rights and Duties Between Friends

Even without a covenant, David and Jonathan would have been bound to show *ḥesed* to one another, since they were friends. *Ḥesed* was the proper conduct of friendship. Each was expected to take heed of the welfare and safety of his friend and to be loyal to him. Friendship also entailed a relationship of mutual rights and duties, as seems to have been the case with any amicable relationship in the ancient Orient. Unwritten laws and binding customs determined every facet of life. Friends were considered brothers, for the concept of brother was a very broad one.[66]

We find *ḥesed*, II Sam. 16:16, 17, as the expected conduct in friendship. When David's friend Ḥushai seemed to have broken faith

[64] Steuernagel, *ibid.*, p. 326.

[65] Steuernagel, *loc. cit.*

[66] W. R. Smith, *Kinship*, p. 14.

with him and called to Absalom: "Long live the King! Long live the king!" even Absalom was surprised and asked Ḥushai: "Is this your loyalty to your friend? Why did you not go with your friend?" Absalom expected as a matter of course that a man would keep faith with his friend, showing him *ḥesed*. In the totality of the concept *ḥesed*, loyalty plays an important part, so that in this passage *ḥesed* might simply be translated as "loyalty."[67] Love, friendship, brotherliness, loyalty, are all inherent in the concept of *ḥesed*. It is possible to do justice to the different shades of meaning only when *ḥesed* is understood as conduct in accordance with a mutual relationship of rights and duties.

Ḥesed should be understood in this sense in II Sam. 10:2 (I Chron. 19:2). David wanted to deal kindly with Ḥanun, as Ḥanun's father had dealt kindly with him. As evidence of his readiness to keep up friendly relations with Ḥanun, he sent envoys to Ḥanun after Naḥash's death to express his condolences and to comfort him. The nature of the friendly relations between David and Naḥash are unknown to us. The origin of their friendship may have been that both of them once fought against Saul,[68] and later, perhaps, it was in their desire to secure peace in Transjordan.[69] The friendship between David and Naḥash was similar to an alliance, even though there was no formal covenant between them. As friends and allies, mutual obligations and rights were incumbent upon both, and both were obligated to show *ḥesed* toward one another; they were not to war against each other and were to be at readiness to lend mutual assistance to one another.

E. *Ḥesed* as the Mutual Relationship of Rights and Duties Between Ruler and Subjects

In the Hebrew Bible, *ḥesed* also denoted the relationship between a ruler and his subject. Between them there existed a condition of mutuality; both assumed obligations and had rights. The loyalty that a subject showed his king had to be reciprocated with loyalty.

1. The King and His Subjects

Ḥesed as conduct in accord with this relationship occurs in II Sam. 3:8. Abner had been in Saul's service and remained on as a general also under Ishbosheth. He was, therefore, obligated to show *ḥesed*

67 Gressmann, *loc. cit.*

68 I Sam. 11:1.

69 Budde, *loc. cit.*

to his king; however, he committed a despicable, humiliating breach of faith by taking possession of Riẓpah, Saul's concubine. For this, Ishbosheth (Ishbaal), as a matter of course, called him to account. In the Orient, it was the custom that the new king took over the harem of his predecessor, announcing thereby to the whole world that he was lord and had assumed all the rights of his predecessor.[70] Abner's action was actually treason. He tried, however, to shrug off the accusation flippantly. He protested his loyalty by addressing Ishbosheth arrogantly, since the latter was totally dependent upon him:

> Am I a (Judean) dog's head? To this day I keep showing loyalty to the house of Saul your father, to his brothers, and to his friends, and have not given you into David's hand; and yet today you charge me with a fault concerning a woman.

The matter, however, was not one to be disposed of so easily. Abner had broken faith with Ishbosheth despite his claim to have practiced and kept *ḥesed.*

In II Chron. 24:22 *ḥesed* appears as true loyalty shown by a subject to his king. There we read that the High Priest Jehoiada always had shown his king, Joash, *ḥesed.* Joash, unmindful of this *ḥesed,* had Jehoiada's son, Zecharia, slain. Joash, who was also otherwise obligated to Jehoiada,[71] therefore committed a breach of faith. Jehoiada's loyalty to Joash, the whole relationship between them, obligated Joash to show *ḥesed* to Jehoiada and his house, since *ḥesed* is based upon mutuality.

2. THE KING AND THOSE WHO SUBMIT TO HIM

Ḥesed is the relationship between the king and one who submits to him, in I Kings 20:31. The Israelite kings had the reputation of being kings who practiced *ḥesed* toward those who had a claim upon it. They were known for their readiness to show *ḥesed* to those who created and fulfilled the basic requirements for establishing such a *ḥesed*-relationship. This reputation, which was in all probability of long standing and had already been proven to be true of David and Solomon,[72] was known to the officers of Benhadad, defeated in battle by Aḥab. They relied upon this trait as the only escape from their otherwise desperate situation, and as a means of saving their king's

[70] Smith, *op. cit.*, p. 89; Gressmann, *op. cit.*, p. 129. II Sam. 16:22; 12:8; I Kings 2:22.

[71] II Chron. 22:11.

[72] Cf. I Kings 2:7; II Sam. 10:2.

life. They well understood that the mutually obligatory *ḥesed*-relationship of rights and duties extended to the relationship between servant and master. Consequently, they girded their loins with sackcloth and tied ropes about their heads. These were the signs of their unconditional surrender and their willingness to submit to the will of the victor. They then approached Aḥab in order to intercede with him for their king, saying: "Your servant Benhadad says, 'Pray, let me live.' "[73] By calling Benhadad a servant of Aḥab, a *ḥesed*-relationship was made possible. Benhadad could hope to remain alive. The usual procedure would have been to have Benhadad slain and this was what was expected by the zealots in Aḥab's camp. But the king generously granted the plea and with political astuteness declared his readiness to establish a *ḥesed*-relationship by answering them: "Does he still live? He is my *brother*."[74] Humanitarian considerations alone would scarcely have prompted Aḥab to save Benhadad from death. Since the latter had submitted himself to him, Aḥab was in the position to show him *ḥesed*. He concluded a pact with him[75] and gave him conditional freedom. Because of this, the reputation of the kings of Israel received new confirmation.

Only in later times does *ḥesed* lose the characteristics of obligation and reciprocity and becomes more like grace and mercy, which is arbitrarily given. In Esther 2:9, 17,[76] *ḥesed* is the favor which the king bestows upon those of his preference, his way of giving aid and assistance to those who are in his grace.[77]

F. *Ḥesed* as Mutual Aid

A mutual relationship also emerged among those who rendered help to one another, even if no other relationship existed between them. He who had been given help was obligated to reciprocate in kind. The helper became his brother; i. e., he had to act toward him as toward a blood relative or ally. On the part of the helper, an act of assistance signified readiness to enter into a mutual relationship, as well as his expectation of being received into such a mutual relationship. He who had been rendered assistance had to recognize the

[73] Vs. 32.

[74] Vs. 32.

[75] Kraetzschmar, *op. cit.*, p. 28. "On the part of Aḥab, the *b^erith* comprised the guarantee of his life and safe conduct, on the part of Benhadad, besides the obligations as in vs. 34, the acknowledgement of the suzerainty of Israel."

[76] נשׂא חסד occurs only in these two verses.

[77] *Supra*, fn. 13.

necessity of acknowledging a mutual relationship and had to act accordingly. The conduct in accord with such a relationship was likewise called *ḥesed.*

Ḥesed of this sort appears in Judg. 1:24. The spies, who were reconnoitering Bethel, requested help from a man they saw emerging from the city. They promised to show him *ḥesed* if he would show them how they could force their way into the city. They assured him that they would reciprocate his aid and, in short, consider him as a member of their group and accord him reciprocal treatment. This they then did. When, under their leadership, the city was later attacked, only that man and his family were spared.[78] "We will deal kindly with you," is the translation of most new commentators. This translation is to be rejected because obligation and reciprocity, which are the constituent qualities of *ḥesed,* are not given expression.

These essentials are clearly recognizable in I Kings 2:7. David ordered his son, Solomon, to consider the members of Barzillai's family as members of his own house, giving them places at his own table; that is, to show them *ḥesed.* Barzillai, the Gileadite, had given help to David when he was fleeing from Absalom; he had received him hospitably and furnished his troops with food and clothing.[79] This act obligated David to consider him as a member of his own family. He did not forget his obligation, and as his death approached, he commanded Solomon to act in accordance with *ḥesed* to Barzillai's family. Modern commentators translate *ḥesed* as "mercy" or "favor," which is unacceptable. The *ḥesed* which Solomon was to show to Barzillai's house did not emanate from mercy but from obligation. It did not depend upon the mere will or whim of David or Solomon, but was a requirement.

In II Sam. 2:5, *ḥesed* appears as the attitude of the recipient of help toward the helper. David blessed the men of Jabesh-gilead for the *ḥesed* they had shown Saul by giving him and his sons a burial after they were slain in the battle against the Philistines.[80] The city of Jabesh-gilead was under an obligation to Saul because he had rescued the city from the Ammonites.[81] Through this act of assistance, a relationship of mutual obligation between Saul and the men of Gilead was created which they readily recognized in that they viewed Saul as their אדון. The *ḥesed* they practiced toward Saul was a service

[78] Vs. 25.

[79] II Sam. 17:27–29; 19:32–41.

[80] Cf. I Sam. 31:11–13; I Chron. 10:11–12.

[81] I Sam. 11:1–11.

of love, in reciprocity for what Saul had done. That *ḥesed* here also embraces אמת is made clear from the following vs. 6. David said to them: "May the Lord show חסד ואמת to you." He hoped that Yahweh would evince toward them the same love and loyalty which they had shown to their ruler, Saul. This means that the men of Jabesh-gilead were addressed as brothers and included in the community of God's faithful, for only those who were elected and stood in a mutually reciprocal relationship with Yahweh could receive חסד ואמת from him.[82]

Judg. 8:35 relates that the people of Israel did not show *ḥesed* to the house of Gideon, although he had performed many acts of kindness for Israel. For this service, loyal reciprocity was owed to him. The people of Israel were under the obligation[83] to show Gideon and his house faithfulness, not only because he was their king but also because he was their deliverer.[84]

In Gen. 40:14 *ḥesed* appears as the reciprocity for help already given. Joseph rendered a great service to the chief butler when he interpreted his dream propitiously. He entreated him that, after his reinstatement to office,[85] he help him and speak to the king on his behalf so that he too might regain freedom. He asked him to act in a manner appropriate to one who has received assistance.

Summary

The previous analysis yields the following conclusions:

A. *Ḥesed* is conduct corresponding to a mutual relationship of rights and duties.

B. *Ḥesed*, when understood as such conduct, explains the previously mentioned fact that only those participating in a mutual relationship of, rights and duties can receive or show *ḥesed*.

[82] Cf. Gen. 24:12, 14, 26, 27; 32:11; Deut. 7:12; Isa. 63:7, 8; Ezra 3:11; Ps. 31:7, 8:89; 148:14; I Kings 8:23; II Chron. 6:14; II Sam. 7:15, 24; I Chron. 17:13, 14; Ps. 18:51; 77:9, 16; 79:2, 13; 106:45, 7; 119:76; 138:2, 8; 143:12; Mic. 7:20. Cf. *supra*, fn. 55.

[83] In Judg. 9:16 Jotham reproaches the Shechemites (which reproach pertains to all of Israel) because they betrayed Gideon, in that they have not dealt with him according to אמת. In Judges 8:35, חסד connotes almost the same meaning as אמת does here and includes אמת. As to Judg. 9:16, cf. Stärk, *op. cit.*, p. 56.

[84] Gressmann, *loc. cit.*, translates *ḥesed* as "loyalty."

[85] Reuss, *loc. cit.*, translates *ḥesed* as "gratitude."

C. *Ḥesed* is conduct in accord with a mutual relationship of rights and duties or conduct corresponding to a mutually obligatory relationship.

1. *Ḥesed* corresponds to the demands of loyalty and includes the concept of *ʾemeth*. The phrase חסד ואמת is then to be regarded as a hendiadys in which אמת is an explanatory adjective.
2. *Ḥesed* can be confirmed by an oath.
3. *Ḥesed* constitutes the essence of a covenant.

D. The component parts of the general concept *ḥesed*, in which the interpretation of *ḥesed* as procedures or performances corresponding to a mutually obligatory relationship, are principally: reciprocity, mutual assistance, sincerity, friendliness, brotherliness, duty, loyalty and love.

E. In the older sources, the common usage of *ḥesed* never means an arbitrary demonstration of grace, kindness, favor or love.

CHAPTER II

Ḥesed as Human Conduct — Its Religious Meaning

I. *ḤESED* IN THE PROPHETIC AND COGNATE LITERATURE AS THE RECIPROCAL CONDUCT OF MEN TOWARD ONE ANOTHER AND EXPLICITLY TOWARD GOD

In the prophetic literature the concept of *ḥesed* was greatly expanded. From the mode of conduct of certain groups standing in a mutual relationship of rights and duties to one another, *ḥesed* becomes the conduct of all men toward one another. This conduct is pleasing to God and is at the same time regarded as the only proper relationship toward God. The dealings of men are considered from a religious point of view and not on the basis of inter-personal relationships alone. The totality of man's life is not sundered from religion but is most intricately intertwined with it, receiving from religion a deeper significance and value. Therefore, one cannot discuss *ḥesed* as the conduct of men corresponding to a reciprocal relationship without looking at *ḥesed* at the same time as the conduct of men toward God.

A. In the Book of Hosea

In order to understand *ḥesed* in the Book of Hosea as a reciprocal relationship among men and as an explicit one toward God, we must briefly analyze the relationship between God and man, and God and Israel, as presented in this book. There is a reciprocal relationship between God and Israel.[1] God provides for His people,[2] grants peace and rest,[3] stands by to help,[4] and is full of benevolence.[5] The people,

[1] Hos. 2:25; 1:9.
[2] Hos. 2:10 f.
[3] Hos. 2:20.
[4] Hos. 12:10.
[5] Hos. 11:3, 4; 3:1.

on the other hand, must obey the divine commandments, heed His demands, and remain faithful in thought and deed. Their duties toward God are the unceasing preservation of the true knowledge of God and continuous adherence to a way of life pleasing to Him. The people must practice משפט, צדקה, אמת and particularly חסד.[6] If the people forsakes its duties, God censures it, and misfortune is the consequence of action in opposition to God's demands.[7] Total obduracy brings with it the risk of rejection.[8]

In Hos. 4:1 we read that God is engaged in litigation with Israel because Israel has not fulfilled the conditions of its relationship to God. The land lacks דעת אלהים, חסד, אמת, loyalty, love and knowledge of God. The words are joined together in ascending significance. *Ḥesed* comprises *ᵓemeth*, and both are contained in *daᶜath ᵓelohim*. The next verse gives the reason why God is angry with His people: there was cursing, lying, theft, adultery, and murder rampant in the land. The reference to the Decalogue is obvious. The people's relationship to God was founded on religious and ethical principles. Ethical conduct was the basis of true religion. Knowledge of God required fidelity and love, both of God and of men toward one another, manifested by the fulfillment of the ethical commandments. A people acting against the demands of *ᵓemeth* and *ḥesed* is also incapable of true knowledge of God.

In Hosea *ḥesed* is a lofty concept, highly refined in the heart of the prophet. It is no longer conduct corresponding to a reciprocal relationship within a narrow circle, but the proper conduct of all men toward one another. On the one hand, mankind is regarded as one large family, and on the other, as children of one heavenly father. The word *ḥesed* signifies man's readiness for mutual aid, stemming from a pure love of humanity; it is the realization of "the generally valid divine commandment of humaneness."[9] *Ḥesed* does not reside in the punctilious offering of sacrifices or in external religiosity, but in ethical and religious behavior and the devoted fulfillment of the divinely ordained ethical commandments. In this respect *ḥesed* as humane conduct is not different from the *ḥesed* of men toward God. True religious motivation is discernible from ethical deeds.[10]

[6] Hos. 4:1; 6:4, 6; 10:12; 12:7.

[7] Hos. 4:1–3; 11:8.

[8] Hos. 9:15 f.; 2:4 f.; 4:6; 5:6.

[9] Wellhausen, *Die Kleinen Propheten* (Berlin, 1898), *ad. loc.*

[10] It is impossible to limit *ḥesed* in chap. 4:1 to a man to man relationship as is done by W. R. Harper (*A Critical and Exegetical Commentary on Amos and Hosea* [Edinburgh, 1910]), *ad. loc.*

It is difficult to translate the word *ḥesed*. "Love" would be correct if one understands under this rubric what has just been said of *ḥesed*. However, for "love" Hosea uses אהבה.[11] Perhaps one could best render *ḥesed* as "religiosity" or "*pietas*."[12]

In Hos. 6:4 God reproaches Israel because its *ḥesed* is inconstant. The people saw in the life of the cultus the truly religious life and did not know what really pleased God. The people had no notion of how they should act in order to gain God's favor. The divine will, however, is clearly expressed in Hos. 6:6: "I desire *ḥesed* and not sacrifice, the knowledge of God, not burnt offerings."[13] In his commentary on Ps. 50, Stärk states what would fit well in this context: "Spiritual service of God and a life of ethical purity — this is God's will for His people. Only he who aspires after this can inherit the kingdom of God."[14] *Ḥesed* and *daᶜath ᵓelohim* are here made parallel. Without *ḥesed* there is no knowledge of God, and a knowledge of God presupposes *ḥesed*. *Ḥesed*[15] is demanded by God, being both man's task and his hope.[16]

In the same sense *ḥesed* also appears in Hos. 10:12 and 12:7.[17] In 10:12 we discover the conditions which Israel has to fulfill in order to come to terms with God. "Sow in justice and you will harvest in *ḥesed*," admonishes the prophet. By practicing justice and charity among themselves, men find the way to God and to their salvation. Only through mutual reciprocity of צדקה and חסד does mankind, in everyday life, manifest the proper attitude and conduct toward God. Only in this way can they find Him and achieve communion with Him.[18]

[11] Hos. 3:1; 9:15; 11:1, 4; 14:5. In Hos. 11:4, Kittel, *B. H.* and Cheyne (*Encyclopaedia Biblica*, p. 2826, fn. 2) want to read חסד for אדם as being a synonym for אהבה. This is unacceptable, for אהבה in Hosea refers to individual love; חסד is reciprocal and obligatory love.

[12] Cf. Wildeboer, *Die Sprüche* (Freiburg i.B., 1897), re chap. 3:3; Harper, *loc. cit.*, re Hos. 10:12.

[13] Cf. I Sam. 15:22 f.; Ps. 50:8; 69:31 f.; Isa. 10:1 f.; 40:16; 66:1 f.; Jer. 7:21 f.; Amos 5:21 f.; Stärk, Die Lyrik² (Göttingen, 1920), p. 136.

[14] Stärk, *op. cit.*, p. 262.

[15] Harper, *loc. cit.*, has recognized here the correct meaning of *ḥesed*. He says that *ḥesed* "is not love for God as distinguished from love for one's fellowmen, but both."

[16] Hos. 2:23–25.

[17] Steuernagel, *op. cit.*, p. 608, "vs. 7 can be an admonition of Hosea addressed to Israel." Cf. also Procksch, *Die kleinen prophetischen Schriften vor dem Exil* (Stuttgart, 1910), *ad. loc.*

[18] Gressmann, *Die älteste Geschichtsschreibung und Prophetie Israels* (Göttingen², 1921), *ad. loc.*

In Hos. 12:7 we read: "So you, by the help of your God, return,[19] keep חסד and משפט, and trust confidently in your God." These words, although addressed to Jacob, may be applied to the whole people of Israel.[20] Its conduct must be in accordance with משפט and חסד before Israel can return to God. Actual ethical action must testify to the inner transformation. *Mishpaṭ* is to be understood in the sense of doing good and hating evil,[21] and *ḥesed* as the ethical and religious conduct of men among themselves, which proves man's obedience to the divine commandments and makes communion between man and God possible.

It is important to point out that in Hosea, too, חסד occurs next to אמת as well as next to צדקה and משפט. *Ḥesed* in the totality of its meaning corresponds to the demands of loyalty, and as divinely ordained conduct, it corresponds at the same time to the demands of justice and righteousness. While אמת, משפט, and צדקה are by no means synonyms for *ḥesed*, they are nevertheless all related to the concept. He who acts in accordance with *ḥesed* will also naturally practice loyalty and righteousness. *Ḥesed*, however, is more than this; it is humaneness and brotherliness toward all. It is the true expression of genuine religiosity.

B. In Other Prophetic Books and Cognate Literature

If one wants to sound the keynote of the Hebrew Bible, it can be expressed as the never-ending striving of genuinely religious men to achieve unity with the will of God. Despite all obstacles, and in the face of all justification for doubt, and in spite of all inclination toward resignation, the truly God-intoxicated man profoundly and bravely says "Yes" to the world and beats a path to God. Walking in God's ways, he strives to find a humble place in the ranks of God's elect. As long as he follows God, God turns to him.[22] There is *ḥesed* between God and the righteous man tied to Him by ethical and religious conduct. Such men are received into His communion. In Jer. 2:2–3 we read:

[19] Procksch, *loc. cit.*; Nowack (*Die Kleinen Propheten* [Göttingen, 1922], *ad. loc.*), among others, translates: "You will return to your tents."

[20] Steuernagel, *op. cit.*, p. 608; cf. Procksch, *loc. cit.*; Gressmann, *op. cit.*, p. 395.

[21] Hertzberg, *Die Entwicklung des Begriffes* משפט *im A. T. Z.A.W.*, Vol. 40, 1922, p. 286.

[22] Cf. *supra*, fn. 20.

> I remember the devotion of your youth,[23] your love as a bride, how you followed Me in the wilderness, in a land not sown. Israel was holy to Yahweh, the first fruits of His harvest. All who ate of it shall rue it; evil shall come upon them.

With true loyalty Israel followed Yahweh through the inhospitable wilderness. Placed on trial, the people passed the test, became קדוש to Yahweh, ראשית תבואתה, and enjoyed his special protection. They achieved communion with God. Practicing *ḥesed*, the people received *ḥesed* from Yahweh. The *ḥesed* which Israel showed Yahweh was the same *ḥesed* that the members of a family were obliged to show toward one another.[24] The *ḥesed* mentioned in our passage is conditioned by אהבת כלולתיך. The *ḥesed* practiced by Israel toward Yahweh was the mutually obligatory relationship of rights and duties in harmony with the family-like relationship between Yahweh and Israel. In this context *ḥesed* cannot be rendered as "graciousness," "affection," "kindness," "favor," or "love," as has been done in various modern commentaries.[25] All these are but peripheral aspects of *ḥesed*, not the core of the concept. Sellin's statements on *ḥesed*, with regard to Hos. 6:6 and Jer. 2:2, are wrong. He says:

> חסד is to Hosea not only as in ancient times the condescension of the superior to an inferior but also courting love, the love of the people for Yahweh who courts them just as in Ruth 3:10, where it speaks of the affection of the young woman for her wooer. Later on, the word was understood in the same sense in Jeremiah 2:2.[26]

Volz[27] and Cheyne[28] come closest to the true meaning of *ḥesed* when they translate חסד נעוריך as "the loyal affection of thy youth." For *ḥesed* was the most important quality the Israelite knew, since it corresponded to the reciprocal relationship of rights and duties. True communality was both a necessity for life and an ideal, and *ḥesed* was the way leading to its fulfillment.[29] This concept was then trans-

[23] Cf. Volz, *Der Prophet Jeremia, ad. loc.*; Torczyner (as per oral communication) reads: "I remembered in your favor. . ."

[24] Cf. Ch. I, pp. 38–43.

[25] Cf. Schmidt, *Die grossen Propheten* (Göttingen, 1923), *ad. loc.*; Reuss, *loc. cit.*; Orelli, *Der Prophet Jeremia* (München, 1905), *ad. loc.*; Duhm, *Das Buch Jeremia* (Tübingen, 1901), *ad. loc.*; Giesebrecht, *Das Buch Jeremia* (Göttingen, 1907), *ad. loc.*; Rothstein (in Kautzsch[4]), *ad. loc.*

[26] Cf. Sellin, *Das Zwölfprophetenbuch* (Leipzig, 1922), p. 53. Cf. particularly my remarks pp. 51–52, pp. 40–43.

[27] Volz, *loc. cit.*

[28] Cheyne, *loc. cit.*

[29] Cf. Ch. I, pp. 38 f.

ferred to the relationship with Yahweh with the sure intuitive knowledge that the holy and the profane constitute one inseparable whole. Through *ḥesed*, communion with Yahweh was sought and made possible.

Mic. 6:8[30] furnishes a striking proof for the use of *ḥesed* in the sense of mutually reciprocal conduct of men among themselves and explicitly *vis-à-vis* God. As in Hosea, the people are again unequivocally told that God has no pleasure in burnt-offerings, and that genuine religiosity does not consist of cultic behavior[31] but rather in the love of one's fellow man, which is the same as faithfulness toward God. We read: "It has been told you, O man, what is good; and what Yahweh requires of you, namely, to do justly, and to love mercy, and to walk humbly with your God."[32] אהבת חסד, משפט and הצנע לכת עם אלהיך are required of men, as is the case in Hos. 4:1 with regard to אמת, חסד and דעת אלהים. Here, as in Hos. 4:1, the words seem to be arranged together in a sequence of ascending significance. Love of humanity[33] includes within it righteous conduct and is already included in an humble attitude toward God. *Ḥesed*, which formerly existed only between those who stood in a fundamentally close relationship toward one another, undergoes considerable expansion in meaning. Every man becomes every other man's brother, *ḥesed* becomes the mutual or reciprocal relationship of all men toward each other and toward God.

In Job 6:14 *ḥesed* is clearly used in the same sense. The text is corrupt and requires emendation: "He who withholds *ḥesed* from his friend forsakes the fear of the Almighty."[34] The *ḥesed* one must practice toward one's friends and fellow men is the basic condition and the first proof of the fear of God. In Prov. 16:1 we read: "By *ḥesed* and

[30] Steuernagel, *op. cit.*, pp. 627–8, thinks that this verse is authentic. Staerk, *Die Entstehung*, p. 98, says: "Micah 6:6–8 is a gospel fragment in the O.T., perhaps a fragment from the seventh century."

[31] Chap. II, fn. 13.

[32] Sellin's translation: "Did men tell you what is good? And what Yahweh requires of you other than . . ." is not acceptable. The verse is not constructed antithetically. If that were the case the whole impact of the command would be lost. As a matter of fact אדם actually refers to Israel and through Israel to all of mankind and cannot be understood as the subject. Sellin suggests the emendation הִכָּנֵעַ for הַצְנֵעַ, but this change is unnecessary. Cf. Sellin, *Das Zwölfprophetenbuch* (Leipzig, 1922), *ad. loc.*

[33] Compare against Orelli, *Die zwölf kleinen Propheten* (München, 1908), *ad. loc.*

[34] Beer, *Der Text des Buches Hiob* (Marburg, 1897), reads מש for מס; Merx, *Das Gedicht von Hiob* (Jena, 1871), reads מנע מרעהו חסד; Hoffmann, *Hiob* (Kiel, 1891), reads למאס for למס.

ʾemeth iniquity is atoned for, and by the fear of the Lord evil is avoided." *Ḥesed* and *ʾemeth* are the distinctive characteristics of the man devoted to the will of God, and make communion with God possible for him. Devotion which is faithful to this communion with God is the essence of fear of the Lord. Whoever has sinned and wishes to achieve atonement with God can, through inner repentance clearly evidenced through deeds of *ḥesed* and *ʾemeth*, regain a worthy place for himself in the community of his fellow men and in the congregation of the Lord.[35]

In Prov. 3:3–4 the teacher of wisdom admonishes the youth: "Let not *ḥesed* and *ʾemeth* forsake you; bind them about your neck, write them on the tablet of your heart, so that you will find favor and good repute[36] in the sight of God and man." He teaches that a person should never consider himself as independent, standing alone, but rather as a member of a community in whose general welfare he seeks his own. By the practice of faithful love, this community becomes the community of all the members of the kingdom of God. It is possible that the teacher of wisdom knew Jer. 31:33, when he admonished his students and listeners to inscribe חסד ואמת on the tablets of their hearts. They are to keep the covenant written by God upon their hearts and to win Him as their God by proving themselves loyal servants through beneficent actions. Children of God, who love God and who are desirous of winning His love, must first begin by practicing divine love among themselves.

In Zech. 7:9 we read that Yahweh says, through the prophet: "Render true judgments, show brotherliness and mercy (חסד ורחמים)!" *Ḥesed* is more than *mishpaṭ ʾemeth*, and from *ḥesed* to *raḥamim* is but a short step. *Ḥesed*, however, embodies the idea of obligation which is not at all the case with *raḥamim*.

In Ps. 109 we have the prayer of a pious man who, in moral indignation, asks God not to show *ḥesed* to his oppressor[37] because the latter never showed *ḥesed*.[38] The oppressor attacked him without reason; persecuted the poor and the afflicted, who are the first to whom one must show *ḥesed*; and disregarded the relationship of trust which has to exist among all men. He also had no love for God. Therefore, according to the worshiper's wish, he should be thrust out of the community and the congregation of the Lord.

We have so far analyzed those passages in which *ḥesed* meant the

[35] Cf. Hos. 12:7; 10:12.
[36] שֵׁם טוב cf. Kittel, *B. H., ad. loc.*
[37] Vs. 12.
[38] Vs. 16.

conduct of men toward one another, corresponding to a reciprocal relationship among men, as well as the conduct of men in relation to God. God demanded *ḥesed* (of men). We now move on to those passages in which *ḥesed* appears as the reciprocal conduct of people toward one another and only implicitly toward God.

II. *ḤESED* IN THE PROPHETIC AND COGNATE LITERATURE AS THE RECIPROCAL CONDUCT OF MEN TOWARD ONE ANOTHER AND IMPLICITLY TOWARD GOD

It is impossible to separate ethics from religion in prophetic and cognate literature.[39] They form a unity and are indissolubly bound together. Hence, in this literature *ḥesed* has direct reference to God, even in those passages which ostensibly only concern themselves with men. The statement of Prov. 3:4, that he who practices *ḥesed* is favored by God and man, is true also of the passages with which we shall deal in this category. These passages make it very clear that the fulfillment of ethical and religious obligations of men brings blessing upon them; that he who acts in accordance with *ḥesed* will be treated in accordance with *ḥesed*.

A. *Ḥesed*-deeds and Their Consequences

1. BY PEOPLE IN GENERAL

In Prov. 11:17 *ḥesed* is clearly revealed in terms of its social character: "A man who practices *ḥesed* benefits himself, but a cruel man cuts into his own flesh."[40] A member of the human family who obeys its laws has the joy and the reward of fulfilling the tasks set by God, of achieving nearness to Him. The individual, however, does not do good calculatedly so as not to fare badly at the hands of others, but rather to live up to the ethical and religious obligations imposed upon him by mankind and the religious community. Consequently, *ḥesed* is shown also to the sick, the poor, and the helpless, who may never be able to reciprocate in kind. According to the beliefs of the ancients, however, a direct relationship between a person's conduct and destiny existed — his righteous conduct would

[39] Volz, *Der Prophet Jeremia* (Leipzig, 1922), p. 294.
[40] Cf. Volz, *Weisheit*, in "Die Schriften des A. T." (Göttingen, 1921), *ad. loc.*

somehow be reciprocated, since this is God's ordained plan for the world.[41] Subjectively understood, *ḥesed*, especially that shown to the poor, may appear as mercy or grace. Objectively, however, *ḥesed* remains the obligatory relationship of men toward one another, and implicitly as well as explicitly toward God. *Ḥesed*, in regard to a deed and its consequences, appears distinctly in Prov. 19:22: "The gain of a man is his *ḥesed*."[42] Here the thought is expressed that blessing and salvation are the portion of one who practices *ḥesed*. *Ḥesed* entails a subtle kind of reward. Whoever views all men as members of his own family, and keeps the welfare of the whole human family before him, creates his own way leading to the kingdom of God (this is not expressed openly but is implied) and will achieve communion with God.

In Prov. 21:21 we read: "He who follows after צדקה and חסד finds חיים, צדקה and כבוד." Apparently, the text speaks here only concerning men; still, *ḥesed* must also relate to God. *Ḥesed*, as the conduct of men toward one another corresponding to a reciprocal relationship, is also the right conduct toward God. The full meaning of the whole sentence is: "He who follows righteousness[43] and brotherliness finds life, justice[44] and honor before God." חסד and צדקה are not synonymous here, for *ḥesed* is richer in meaning.[45] *Ẓ*ᵉ*dakah* means right conduct, and in this passage perhaps even more. *Ḥesed* is conduct corresponding to a reciprocal relationship, brotherliness, and love in general. In its response to the demands of doing right, *ḥesed* naturally encompasses *ẓ*ᵉ*dakah*. The difference in meaning between *ẓ*ᵉ*dakah* and *ḥesed* gradually diminishes so that *ẓ*ᵉ*dakah* is absorbed in the meaning of *ḥesed*.[46] A צדיק and an איש חסד are one and the same,[47] the *ẓadik* practices *ḥesed*.[48]

Ḥesed, in relation to action and consequence, also occurs in Prov. 14:22: "Indeed, those who devise evil come to error, but those who devise good have *ḥesed* and ᵓ*emeth* as recompense." Here the thought

[41] Prov. 19:17: "He that helps the poor lends to God; He will repay him his good deed."

[42] Read תבואת for תאות. Cf. Kittel, *B. H., ad. loc.*, Wildeboer, *loc. cit.*, Frankenberg, *Die Sprüche* (Göttingen, 1898), *ad. loc., passim.*

[43] Kautzsch, *Über die Derivate des Stammes* צדק *im Alttestamentlichen Sprachgebrauche* (Tübingen, 1881), p. 144.

[44] *Ibid.*, p. 49.

[45] Cf. Ch. II, pp. 58–59; Isa. 16:5; Jer. 9:23; Ps. 33:5; 40:11, 12; 85:11; 89:15; 36:11; 103:17, 18; 145:17.

[46] Cf. Dalman, *Die richterliche Gerechtigkeit im A. T.* (Berlin, 1897), p. 7, fn. 6.

[47] Isa. 57:1.

[48] Ps. 141:5; cf. Prov. 27:6.

remains unexpressed that those who practice goodness may expect like conduct from God. Those who fulfill the obligations of human society and of God's covenantal community shall enjoy their prerogatives and rights. However, those who do wickedly forfeit their rights in human society and will be excluded from God's covenantal community as well. Whoever wishes to experience *ḥesed* and *ʾemeth* must first practice *ḥesed* and *ʾemeth.*

It is the glory of the woman of valor that she acts according to *ḥesed.* In the beautiful thirty-first chapter of Proverbs, v. 26, she is praised with the words: "She opens her mouth with wisdom and the teaching of kindness (תורת חסד) is on her tongue." The woman of valor speaks and acts with love. That a lesson taught with loving kindness is valuable and spiritually useful can be discerned from Ps. 141:5: "Out of kindness a good man strikes me and rebukes me."

2. BY RULERS

In Prov. 20:28 we read that a king must build his throne on *ḥesed* if it is to endure. For the *ḥesed* which a king practices ensures him the *ḥesed* and the *ʾemeth* of his subjects and, it goes without saying, of his God, to whom he pays homage.[49] The duties of the king, as ruler, are identical with the religious and ethical obligations, the fulfillment of which will make his realm endure.[50] We would like to translate the verse: "Love and loyalty will protect the king if he builds his throne on love."[51] It has been proposed to read with the Septuagint צדק for the second חסד in the verse,[52] such as in Isa. 9:6 and Prov. 16:12; this, however, is unnecessary. *Ḥesed* already encompasses צדק, and there is no need to change the text.

In Isa. 16:5 it is likewise possible to understand *ḥesed* as the ethical and religious conduct of a king:[53] "Then a throne will be established in steadfast love and on it will sit in faithfulness in the tent of David a judge who seeks justice and is quick to do righteousness." In ancient times *ḥesed* was the conduct prescribed by the mutual relationship of rights and duties between king and people. Here, as in Prov. 20:28, *ḥesed* signifies more: it is the conduct of the king, as a servant of the Lord, toward his subjects.

[49] Ps. 61:8. [50] Prov. 29:14.

[51] Frankenberg, *loc. cit.*; Strack, *Die Sprüche Salomos* (Nördlingen, 1888), *ad. loc.*, suggests the translation "Die Ausübung von *ḥesed* und *ʾemeth*. . . ."

[52] Cf. Kittel, *B. H.*, *ad. loc.*; Torczyner (oral communication).

[53] Also Dillmann, *Der Prophet Jesaia* (Leipzig, 1890), *ad. loc.*; Orelli, *Der Prophet Jesaia* (München, 1904), *ad. loc.*

Ḥesed is also to be understood in this sense in Ps. 101:1: "I will sing of loyalty and of justice, to thee, O Lord, I will sing praises." A king presents "the religious and ethical tenets of his rule,"[54] namely — *ḥesed* and *mishpaṭ*. *Ḥesed* is the love which is identical with the demands of law and justice; it unites the members of a group. The love and justice which men practice toward one another give implicit evidence of their proper attitude toward God. It is in this way that verse 1b is to be understood. This is the interpretation of Kessler and Baethgen.[55] Kessler says: "The further content of the psalm shows that *ḥesed* and *mishpaṭ* refer to a human relationship." On the other hand, according to verse 1b, the poem is in praise of Yahweh. Both are unified if one considers that, through *ḥesed* and *mishpaṭ*, we have conduct prescribed by God which corresponds to a divine quality and relationship, which may likewise be expressed through *ḥesed* and *mishpaṭ*.

We saw in this chapter that *ḥesed* is the conduct of men toward one another, which corresponds to a reciprocal relationship. Explicitly as well as implicitly, it is also the proper relationship of men toward God, which implies that *ḥesed* is at one and the same time in accord with the demands of morality and of true religion. Before concluding our analysis of *ḥesed*, as used in this sense, we shall still have to look at those passages in which *ḥesed* occurs particularly between man and man.

III. THE *ḤASID*

A. As the Opposite of the Sinner

The *ḥasid* is the faithful servant of the Lord[56] who gains communion with Him because he has proved himself worthy, through ethical and religious conduct. He relies on God.[57] He practices justice, shows loyalty and love, and orders his daily life according to the divinely ordained ethical commandments. In Ps. 37:28, as in Ps. 97:10 and I Sam. 2:9,[58] the *ḥasid* is contrasted with the wicked and the godless;[59] he enjoys the love of God, while the sinner faces extinc-

[54] Staerk, Lyrik², p. 256.

[55] Kessler, *Die Psalmen* (München, 1899), *ad. loc.*; Baethgen, *Die Psalmen* (Göttingen, 1904), *ad. loc.*

[56] Cf. Ps. 86:2; 79:2; 143:12; 119:124; 31:17; II Chron. 6:41, 42.

[57] Cf. Ch. II, fn. 56; Ps. 32:6; 145:10; 30:45; Neh. 13:14.

[58] Ehrlich, *Randglossen zur Hebräischen Bibel* (Leipzig, 1910), Vol. III, *ad. loc.*, reads מעגלי חסידיו יאיר for רגלי חסידיו ישמר.

[59] Ps. 52:3.

tion.[60] In Prov. 11:17 the איש חסד is the opposite of the אכזרי, the heartless.

B. Identical With the Honest and the Just

Through Ps. 18:26 and II Sam. 22:26 we see that the *ḥasid* is the same as the גבר תמים, the upright man. In Mic. 7:2 ישר באדם, the just man, is equated with the *ḥasid* as are the ישרים and the הלכי תם to the *ḥasidim* in Prov. 2:8. In Isa. 57:1 צדיק is parallel to אנשי חסד.

C. Identical With the Faithful

In Prov. 20:6 איש חסד is parallel to איש אמונים.[61] To understand איש חסד in this verse, as one who merely makes fair promises but is not a responsible person,[62] totally contradicts *ḥesed*'s essence. Inextricably intertwined with חסד are אמת and אמונה.[63] Consequently, an איש חסד must also be an איש אמונים.[64] As Frankenberg correctly notes, he is "not a man who holds out prospects and makes promises leaving the one concerned in a lurch, but who actually performs acts of charity and is loyal, pious, and charitable."[65] This verse points up the vast difference between mere assertion and action; not everyone who has the reputation of being a *ḥasid* necessarily is one.[66] Only he is a *ḥasid* who is an איש אמונים, who comports himself with his neighbor and God in loyalty, by showing *ḥesed*. God cares for him, protects him and enables him to participate in His sacred[67] community. With great zeal, He fulfills the promise made to those who are loyal to Him, just as they had been zealous in fulfilling His commandments, through ethical and religious deeds. To the *ḥasid*, He shows Himself as a *ḥasid*.[68]

[60] In Ps. 27:28 read עולים נשמדו for לעולם נשמְרו. Cf. Staerk, *loc. cit.*; Kittel, *B. H.*, *ad. loc.*

[61] In agreement with Luther, Beer in Kittel's *B. H.* and others read יִקָרא איש הסד for יקרא איש חסדו. If the text is to remain unchanged, translate with Frankenberg, *loc. cit.*, "Many men boast, each of his *ḥesed*, but who may find one who speaks the truth."

[62] Delitzsch, *Das Salomonische Spruchbuch* (Leipzig, 1873), *ad. loc.*; Strack, *loc. cit.*; Wildeboer, *loc. cit.*

[63] Cf. Frankenberg, *loc. cit.*; Gen. 21:23; 47:29; Josh. 2:14; II Sam. 2:6; Hos. 4:1; Prov. 3:3; 14:22; 16:6.

[64] Cf. Ps. 31:24; 12:2.

[65] Frankenberg, *loc. cit.*

[66] This reminds one of Ibsen's *Pillars of Society*.

[67] Cf. Ps. 97:10; 37:28; I Sam. 2:9; Ps. 85:9; 16:10; 31:24; 43:1; 52:11; 116:15; 132:9, 16; 148:14; 86:2; 149; 89:20.

[68] Cf. Ps. 145:17; 18:26; II Sam. 22:26; Jer. 3:12.

The relationship between God and people was one of mutual rights and duties with *ḥesed* as the norm of conduct. It was a covenant-alliance based on *ḥesed* and existing because of *ḥesed* exactly as in the case of a secular alliance.[69] The relationship could be maintained only as long as *ḥesed* was mutually practiced. *Ḥesed* was also to be viewed as a task whose completion must always remain a distant goal. The obligations of the members of the alliance never ended; their mutual rights were valid for all times. Only he who practiced *ḥesed* could receive *ḥesed* from his ally. We saw that it is only toward the *ḥasid* that God acts as a *ḥasid*.[70] Whoever was a *ḥasid* could remain such only so long as he consistently proved himself a *ḥasid*. This was the meaning of Prov. 20:6,[71] and this is also the meaning of Ps. 50:5. The close connection between *ḥesed* and *bᵉrith* is clearly in evidence in this verse, for חסידי is parallel with כרתי בריתי. However, this does not mean that *ḥesed* is a synonym for *bᵉrith*, as Elbogen maintains.[72] *Ḥesed* is the premise and effect of a *bᵉrith*; it constitutes the very essence of a *bᵉrith* but is not yet a *bᵉrith*, even though there can be no *bᵉrith* without *ḥesed*.[73] The *ḥasidim* fulfill their covenantal obligations in that they practice *ḥesed* and may, for this reason, be designated as כרתי בריתי. In Ps. 50:5 they are the members of the divine covenant[74] who are under obligation to abide by the covenant made with God. There is a clear allusion here to the Sinaitic covenant found in Exod. 24:5 f. The *ḥasidim* are taken to task and censured for having failed to uphold the ethical and religious conditions of the covenant, and not because they have been lax in offering sacrifices. For the latter, God could not care less.[75] He who is superficially religious but in fact a moral reprobate, neglectful of the ethical Decalogue, ought not dare to enumerate the statutes of the Lord and talk about His covenant.[76] Elbogen correctly remarks[77] that, in view of the rebuke administered to the *ḥasidim*, the expression "my faithful" (the usual translation for חסידי being "my faithful ones") would have been intended ironically. This, however, does not fit the prophetic tone of the author. If God had recognized the *ḥasidim* as His faithful, it would have been wrong for Him to reproach them for their lack of true piety. The *ḥasidim* referred to here, as Kittel pointedly remarks,

[69] Cf. Ch. I, pp. 46 ff.

[70] Cf. *supra*, fn. 68.

[71] Cf. p. 67.

[72] Elbogen, *loc. cit.*

[73] Cf. Ch. I, pp. 46 ff.

[74] Cf. Elbogen, *loc. cit.*

[75] Vss. 8–13.

[76] Vss. 16–20.

[77] Elbogen, *loc. cit.*

are "the people, not called so for its actual goodness, for that is contested, but for its true relationship to Yahweh."[78] They are God's allies and they can keep up their relationship with Him only by perpetually fulfilling His ethical commandments. They can be, and remain, *ḥasidim* only as long as they comport themselves according to the sacred covenant concluded at Sinai and as long as they practice *ḥesed*.

We have seen that *ḥesed* corresponds to the demands of loyalty, of justice and of righteousness. The *ḥasid*, the *ḥesed*-practicing individual, fulfills the demands of loyalty, of righteousness and of love. His attitude toward men and God is in accord with society and the Lord's covenantal community.

Summary

From the preceding investigation we conclude the following:

A. *Ḥesed* is practiced mutually by all men, as co-equal members of human society.

B. *Ḥesed* is the reciprocal conduct of men toward one another and, at the same time, explicitly and implicitly, the proper relationship toward God. These two aspects of *ḥesed* are inseparable.

C. As reciprocal ethical and religious conduct, *ḥesed* fulfills the demands of loyalty, justice, righteousness, and honesty. These concepts are embraced in its meaning.

D. *Ḥesed* is embodied in the concepts "knowledge of God" and "fear of God" and can be used synonymously for them.

E. The meaning of *ḥesed* can best be translated as religiosity, piety, kindness, and love of mankind.

F. *Ḥesed* is very closely related to the concept of mercy, but is distinguished from it in that *ḥesed* is obligatory.

G. Subjectively understood, *ḥesed* can appear as favor, mercy, compassion. Objectively, *ḥesed* remains obligatory, determined by the divinely-based ethical commandments which are the laws of human society.

H. The *ḥasid*, as one who practices *ḥesed*, is similarly defined.

I. *Ḥesed*, as human conduct in the ethical and religious sense, occurs only in the prophetic and related literature.

[78] Kittel, *Die Psalmen* (Leipzig, 1922), *ad. loc.*

CHAPTER III

Ḥesed as Divine Conduct

I. ḤESED AS THE RECIPROCAL RELATIONSHIP OF GOD TO THE PATRIARCHS

In Gen. 24 we read of the journey which Abraham's steward made to Mesopotamia, where Abraham's relatives lived,[1] in order to choose a wife for Isaac. He stopped in the town where Naḥor,[2] Abraham's brother,[3] dwelt. The steward entreated God to show *ḥesed* to his master by helping him to fulfill the task set by Abraham. "And he said: 'O Yahweh, the God of my master Abraham, grant me good luck today, and show *ḥesed* to my master Abraham.'" (Gen. 24:12) He asked Yahweh to let him know whether he would really show *ḥesed* to Abraham.

> So, I will stand by the spring while the daughters of the townsmen come out to draw water. Let it be, that the maiden to whom I will say, "Please, lower your jar, that I may drink," and who says, "Drink, and I will also water your camels," she will be the one that you have appointed for your servant Isaac. By this I shall know that you have shown *ḥesed* to my master.[4] (Gen. 24:13–14)

Everything happened as he had imagined it. When he learned the name of the gracious girl, he thanked Yahweh for having led Rebecca,[5] Abraham's niece, to him, to be affianced as Isaac's wife.

[1] Cf. Procksch, *Die Genesis*, re chap. 24:7; König, *Die Genesis*, p. 454, fn. 1.

[2] The name of the town was Ḥaran. Cf. Gen. 11:31; 12:5; 27:43; 28:10; König, *ibid.*, re chap. 24:10.

[3] Cf. Gen. 22:20–23; 24:15, 24, 47–48.

[4] Procksch, *loc. cit.*, assigns vss. 13–14 a b^{α} to E and vs. $14^{b\beta}$ as well as vs. 12 to H. Gunkel, in *Die Urgeschichte und die Patriarchen, ad. loc.*, also distinguishes in chap. 24 two different recensions, J^a and J^b, and likewise assigns vss. 13–14 a b^{α} to the second one, J^b, and like Procksch lets vs. 14 b^{β} follow upon vs. 12. It is an interruption which leaves vs. 14 b^{β}, so to speak, suspended in mid-air. How is the servant to recognize that Yahweh had shown *ḥesed* to his master if not in the manner suggested by him in vss. 13–14 a b^{α}?

[5] Cf. *supra*, fn. 3; Holzinger in Kautzsch, *Die Heilige Schrift*[4], p. 46, fn. b

> And he said, "Blessed be Yahweh, the God of my master Abraham, who has not withheld his *ḥesed* and his faithfulness from my master. For[6] Yahweh has led me on the right road[7] to the house of my master's kinsmen."[8] (Gen. 24:27)

In these passages *ḥesed* is something which is due to Abraham and which Abraham's servant expects and asks for from Yahweh because of the special relationship between Yahweh and his master. When praying to Yahweh to show Abraham *ḥesed* or in thanking him for it, he addresses Yahweh as "the God of my master Abraham."[9] Gunkel correctly states: "It is customary to include in the prayer of the worshiper certain predicates of God that justify the request of the worshiper."[10] Yahweh was the God of Abraham; Abraham was his servant.[11] Theirs was a very distinct relationship which imposed upon them certain rights and duties — a relationship of mutual reciprocity expressed by *ḥesed*. This relationship was different from a purely secular one, not in its premises or consequences, but by the nature of the two parties involved. By the same right with which Abraham's servant could demand *ḥesed* and *ᵓemeth* for his master from his relatives,[12] he could also ask Yahweh to help him, and through him Abraham, by showing the latter *ḥesed*. The basis for the mutuality between Abraham and Rebecca's family was consanguinity. The basis for the relationship between Yahweh and Abraham was God's act of choosing Abraham and his promise to aid Abraham and his offspring.[13] (*Ḥesed* is also mentioned in connection with Yahweh's covenant with the Patriarchs, as will be shown later.)[14] Both alliances put upon the participants the obligation to exercise *ḥesed* mutually. The *ḥesed* of Yahweh is, therefore, not to be understood as "grace," "favor," or "kindness," but as the covenantal relationship between him and Abraham. In verse 27, as in verse 49, חסד ואמת are to be re-

[6] Cf. *B. H.*; Procksch, *loc. cit.*

[7] Cf. vs. 48, according to which one should perhaps read here בדרך אמת; Procksch, *loc. cit.*

[8] Cf. *B. H.*; Gunkel, *loc. cit.*; Holzinger, *loc. cit.*

[9] Vss. 12, 27, 42, 48.

[10] Gunkel, *Genesis* (Göttingen, 1910), p. 253.

[11] Cf. Ps. 105:6, 42; Isa. 41:8.

[12] Cf. vs. 49; Ch. I, pp. 11–12.

[13] Cf. Gen. 24:7; 12:1–3; 26:24; 32:10–13; 28:13–16; 31:3; Ps. 105:42; Mic. 7:20. Regarding Gen. 24:7, cf. Procksch, *op. cit.*, p. 141. He says: "ואשר דבר לי and ואשר נשבע לי seem to be variants of which the one with נשבע is deuteronomic and stems from R, where the oath of God is emphasized."

[14] Cf. Kraetzschmar, *op. cit.*, pp. 143 f. Gen. 15:18; 17:2 f.; Exod. 6:4; Lev. 26:42; Deut. 4:31; 7:12; Ps. 105:8 f.; Ch. III, pp. 73 ff.

garded as hendiadys, in which ᵓ*emeth* has the value of an explanatory adjective. Wherever *ḥesed* appears together with ᵓ*emeth* or ᵓ*emunah*, the quality of loyalty inherent in the concept *ḥesed* is emphasized.[15] The servant praises Yahweh who had faithfully shown *ḥesed* toward Abraham. In verse 48 he also speaks of the "way of loyalty"[16] by which Yahweh had guided him in the fulfillment of his request. Yahweh's covenant-based loyalty (gemeinschaftgemässe Treue) naturally presupposed Abraham's loyalty to him.[17]

In Gen. 32:11 *ḥesed* occurs also in connection with ᵓ*emeth*. In his plea to Yahweh for protection from Esau (Gen. 32:10–13), Jacob humbly rendered thanks for the loyal assistance he had already received from Yahweh. He says in verse 11a: "I am not worthy of all the *ḥasadim*[18] and of all the loyalty which you have shown to your servant." Just as Abraham's servant first referred to the relationship between Yahweh and Abraham by addressing him as "God of my master Abraham," thereby establishing his claim to the fulfillment of his prayer, so Jacob addressed God in verse 10 as "God of my father Abraham and God of my father Isaac," and thanked him for the *ḥesed* shown him in the past when praying to him for deliverance from danger. Implicitly, he uses this as the basis for his hope in Yahweh showing *ḥesed* and ᵓ*emeth* in the future.[19] In verse 11 he also refers to the promise[20] upon which the relationship between Yahweh and his fathers is founded and calls himself Yahweh's servant.[21] In everyday life *ḥesed* was the reciprocal conduct expected in the relationship between master and servant.[22] Similarly, *ḥesed* characterizes the reciprocal relationship between Yahweh and his servants. Yahweh keeps his promise and consequently shows *ḥesed* to those who walk

[15] Cf. Ch. I, pp. 43, 47, 54; Ch. III, p. 35; Gen. 32:11; 47:29; Exod. 34:6; Deut. 7:9; II Sam. 2:6; 7:15–16; 15:20; Josh. 2:14; Isa. 55:3; Hos. 2:21–22; 4:1; Mic. 7:20; Ps. 25:10; 26:3; 31:24; 36:6: 40:11–12; 57:4, 11; 61:8; 69:14; 77:9; 85:11; 86:15; 88:12; 89:2, 3, 15, 25, 29, 34, 50; 92:3; 98:3; 100:5; 115:1; 117:2; 119:41; 138:2; Prov. 3:3; 14:22; 16:6; 20:6; 20:28; Lam. 3:22–23.

[16] Procksch, *loc. cit.*

[17] Cf. the two narratives, Gen. 22:1–14; 19:15–18.

[18] Like LXX and in agreement with Procksch, *loc. cit.*, it is also possible to read חסד instead of חסדים. He explains the ים' in חסדים as a cacography of the ום in the following word ומכל. Cf. also Reuss, *loc. cit.*; Gunkel, *loc. cit.*

[19] Gunkel, *ibid.*, p. 358: "This prayer of thanksgiving also contains a consolation: God who helped so often will not forsake His faithful in this instance either."

[20] Cf. *infra*, fn. 30, p. 73.

[21] Cf. vs. 11; *infra*, fn. 28.

[22] Cf. Ch. I, pp. 51–52.

before him.[23] *Ḥasadim* are the reciprocal acts which Yahweh performed, in his faithfulness, to his servant Jacob.

In Mic. 7:20 the hope is expressed that Yahweh will keep the *ᵓemeth* and *ḥesed* he swore to Jacob and Abraham. Jacob and Abraham signify all of Israel.[24] *Ḥesed*, in connection with *ᵓemeth*, always means an attitude of mutual loyalty. The relationship created by God's oath required the practice of *ḥesed* and *ᵓemeth*. They are, as Nowack says, "the essential content of the promise."[25] Thus *ḥesed* can be translated as "loyalty" and also as "love" so as to emphasize that it is Yahweh's *ḥesed*. However, one must remain aware that a very particular kind of "love" is meant, conforming to loyalty and obligation and thereby fulfilling the conditions of the covenant.

Ps. 98:3 speaks of the *ḥesed* and *ᵓemunah* of Yahweh toward Jacob[26] and Israel. "He has remembered his avowed loyalty to 'Jacob'; His faithfulness to the house of Israel. The ends of the earth have seen the victory of our God."[27] With full faith in the actualization of *Yahweh's* promise, the writer describes the expected *ḥesed* and *ᵓemunah* due, in accordance with faithful covenantal loyalty, as if the event were already in the past. It is hardly an accident that verse 3b mentions *Yahweh's* "victory." Further, in verse 2 we read: "Yahweh has made known his victory, he has revealed his vindication in the sight of nations." ישועה and צדקה (meant in the sense of the covenantal relationship of Yahweh toward all the people of Israel)[28] are the acts by which Yahweh shows his *ḥesed* and *ᵓemunah* in history.[29]

Deut. 7:12[30] makes mention of the *bᵉrith* and the ensuing *ḥesed* sworn by Yahweh to the patriarchs. The covenant[31] concluded between Yahweh and the patriarchs, established through an oath, had *ḥesed* as a consequence. *Ḥesed* was the content of every *bᵉrith* as well

[23] *Infra*, fn. 156, p. 89.

[24] Nowack, *Die Kleinen Propheten, ad. loc.*, says: "אברהם just like יעקב personifies the nation descended from him."

[25] Nowack, *loc. cit.*

[26] Cf. *B. H.*; Briggs, *A Critical and Exegetical Commentary on the Book of Psalms* (Edinburgh, 1916), *ad. loc.*; Staerk, *loc. cit.*

[27] Staerk, *loc. cit.*

[28] Kautzsch, *Über die Derivate des Stammes* צדק *im Alttestamentlichen Sprachgebrauch*, p. 45.

[29] Cf. Ch. II, pp. 59, 61–62, 64–65, 65–66. Ps. 6:5; 13:6; 17:7; 18:51; II Sam. 22:51; Ps. 31:17; 33:5; 40:11–12; 57:4; 69:14; 85:8; 86:2; 119:41; 132:9, 16; II Chron. 6:41; Hos. 2:21; Jer. 9:23; Ps. 33:5; 36:11; 85:11, 15; 103:17–18; 145:17.

[30] Cf. Deut. 7:9; Neh. 1:5; 9:32; Dan. 9:4; I Kings 8:23; II Chron. 6:14.

[31] Cf. *supra*, fn. 14, p. 71.

as every covenantal relationship.[32] *Ḥesed, per se,* could also be the object of an oath.[33] The fundamental relationship among the terms ברית, חסד and שבועה is also attested to in Jewish liturgy, in the *Zichronoth* prayer for the new year.[34] Elbogen alludes to this.[35] In the liturgy we read:

וקיים לנו . . . את הברית ואת החסד ואת השבועה אשר נשבעת לאברהם

Ḥesed is contained in *b^erith*[36] and, like a *b^erith*, it could be established by an oath, as is attested to in this passage.[37] ברית, חסד and שבועה are closely related to one another and, therefore, are synonymous,[38] since they express — and this is the significance of their juxtaposition — Yahweh's acceptance of Abraham and his descendants into the covenant.

[32] The arguments given by Kraetzschmar (*op. cit.*, pp. 145–6) as to why חסד was put beside ברית, are wrong. He says: "Accordingly, the divine mercy (חסד) which depended on Yahweh's will alone was not regarded as a sufficient guarantee for the continuance of his favor. The extremely strong guilt feelings which appeared during the 7th century necessitated a stronger support against God's punishing justice than the concept *ḥesed* would offer. In addition, the progressive removal of the deity into the heights of a transcendental world which threatened to become inaccessible to men made it necessary to find a firm buttress which made man certain of the enduring nearness of God despite his transcendence. These supports were supplied by the concept of the *b^erith* existing between God and Israel. It was something to which one could appeal, in the face of God's wrath as well as in petitions for help." Against this, it may be remarked that חסד was put beside ברית because it belongs there and constitutes the contents of ברית. *Ḥesed*, as well as *b^erith*, secures the continuance of the divine favor as long as the people fulfills the obligations of the covenant. Neither *b^erith* nor *ḥesed* can prevail against the punishing justice of God. Cf. Ps. 89:31–38; II Sam. 7:14–15. There is no other expression in the Old Testament which, as our investigation shows, expresses as definitely as *ḥesed* the closest partnership relation between God and his faithful, and it was precisely to this that the faithful appealed in their prayers for help.

In contrast to Kraetzschmar, Driver (*A Critical and Exegetical Commentary on Deuteronomy* [Edinburgh, 1912], on Deut. 7:9) understood the nature of *ḥesed* correctly. He says: "*Ḥesed* is a wider and a more comprehensive term than 'mercy'; 'mercy' is properly the quality by which a person renounces, out of motives of benevolence or compassion, his legitimate rights against one, for instance, who has offended or injured him; but *ḥesed* is a quality exercised mutually among equals; it is the kindliness of feeling, consideration, and courtesy, which adds a grace and softness to the relations subsisting between members of the same society."

[33] Cf. Ch. I, pp. 39, 45, 47–49.

[34] Elbogen, *Der jüdische Gottesdienst in seiner geschichtlichen Entwicklung* (Leipzig, 1924), pp. 141 f.

[35] Elbogen, חסד — *Verpflichtung, Verheissung, Bekräftigung*, p. 44.

[36] Cf. Ch. I, pp. 46 f.

[37] Deut. 7:8–9.

[38] Elbogen, *loc. cit.*

The phrase at the beginning of the *sh'moneh ᶜesre,*

וזוכר חסדי אבות ומביא גואל לבני בניהם

to which Elbogen makes reference,[39] must be translated: "He (the God of Abraham, Isaac and Jacob) remembers the faithfulness sworn to the fathers in the covenant, and brings the redeemer for their children's children." It could also be translated: "God remembers the covenant[40] with the fathers . . ." Elbogen here renders חסדי[41] as "covenant."[42] The preceding words, גומל חסדים טובים,[43] form a close connection with וזוכר חסדי אבות. God remembers the *ḥesed* he swore to the fathers and brings salvation to their descendants' children (the implicit hope is thereby expressed that it shall remain so in the future). He is first called the God who repays the חסדים, the deeds resulting from the reciprocal relationship of his faithful,[44] by exercising *ḥesed* toward them.

II. *ḤESED* AS THE RECIPROCAL RELATIONSHIP OF GOD TO DAVID AND HIS HOUSE

Yahweh promises David (II Sam. 7) to show *ḥesed* to his descendants. We read in verses 14–16 (I Chron. 17:13–14):

> I will be his father, and he shall be my son. When he commits iniquity, I will chasten him with the rod of men, with the stripes of the sons of men; but I will not take away my *ḥesed* from him, as I took it from Saul, whom I put away from before you. And your house and your kingdom shall be made sure forever before me; your throne shall be established forever.[45]

The very fact of Yahweh's choosing David,[46] after having rejected Saul, created a relationship entailing *ḥesed.* (In Ps. 132:11–12 mention is made of the oath Yahweh swore to David to maintain his throne

[39] Elbogen, *ibid.*, pp. 45–46.

[40] Cf. Ch. III, pp. 77–79.

[41] Elbogen, *loc. cit.*, remarks: חסדי אבות is *genitivus objectivus* like חסדי דוד in Isa. 55:3.

[42] Elbogen, *ibid.*

[43] Elbogen, *ibid.*, p. 46, fn. 1, says: "גומל חסדים טובים is a gloss probably added here for the purpose of using חסדים also in another meaning as a stylistic refinement." Cf. Elbogen, *Der jüdische Gottesdienst*, pp. 27, 43.

[44] Cf. Ps. 13:6; Isa. 63:7; Prov. 11:17; 19:17; Ps. 62:13.

[45] Cf. Gressmann, *Die älteste Geschichtsschreibung, ad. loc.*; Kittel in *H. S.*[4], *ad. loc.*

[46] Cf. Ch. I, pp. 42 f.

faithfully, if his descendants would keep the divine covenant.) Yahweh explains, and at the same time strengthens, his promise when he says the relationship between him and David's descendants is to be the same as between father and son. The relationship between father and son was, as is known, a mutual relationship of rights and duties,[47] which made necessary the reciprocal practice of *ḥesed*. As Kittel remarks, David's descendants were to be Yahweh's sons "in an ethical sense." "God is considered father and he as God's son, and this entails ethical obligations."[48] Yahweh's ethical demands could not have been emphasized more strongly, and his own obligations could not have been more emphatically underscored. A father would never withhold his *ḥesed* from his sons; if he did so, he would not be a father. It is self-evident that the sons had to comport themselves with *ḥesed* to the father, otherwise they would risk punishment.

In Ps. 89 the contents of II Sam. 7:14–16 are repeated almost verbatim in poetic form.[49] The author, who bases his entire poem on God's *ḥesed*, stressed every aspect of the relationship between Yahweh and David, which made the practicing of *ḥesed* both possible and necessary. Yahweh swore by his faithfulness to show David *ḥesed*,[50] by designating the relationship between himself and David as that which exists between a father and his first-born.[51] He committed himself to the obligation involved in his promise to show *ḥesed* to David and his descendants, as was called for in the covenantal relationship existing between them. This *ḥesed* was one with God's faithfulness, as is evident in several places in Ps. 89.[52] In verse 34,[53] Yahweh says that he will not withhold his *ḥesed* or break his loyalty with David's descendants. In this connection we recall Gen. 21:23 where שקר is the opposite of חסד.[54] *Ḥesed*, in Ps. 89, is parallel not only to *ᵓemunah*, or *ᵓemeth*, but also to *bᵉrith* — and herein lies the essential difference between Ps. 89 and II Sam. 7:14–16. We read in Ps. 89:29: "My *ḥesed* I will keep for him for ever, and my *bᵉrith* will remain firm for him." This parallelism can be understood only if it is recognized that *Yahweh's* promise to show David's house *ḥesed* is identified in Ps. 89 with *bᵉrith*. Parallel to נשבעתי לדוד עבדי in verse 4b

[47] I Sam. 10–11, 23.
[48] Kittel in *H. S.*⁴, p. 462, fn. "c."
[49] Vss. 25, 27–28, 31–34.
[50] Cf. vss. 50, 25, 34; Ps. 132:11–12.
[51] Vss. 27–28.
[52] Vss. 2, 3, 25, 34, 50, 15.
[53] Vs. 36.
[54] Cf. Ch. I, p. 45.

we find in verse 4a כרתי ברית לבחירי. We learn from verse 50 that it was *ḥesed* to which Yahweh had sworn and it was *ḥesed* which was the actual substance of the covenant:

איה חסדיך הראשנים אדני נשבעת לדוד באמונתך

Although the parallel in verse 29 between *ḥesed* and *b^e^rith* evidences that the two concepts are related, they are still not identical in meaning. *Ḥesed* is the result of a *b^e^rith* relationship, as of any other relationship, and to that extent distinct from *b^e^rith*. However, since *b^e^rith* and *ḥesed*, above all, express the idea of covenant, the difference in meaning is, for practical purposes, only a formal one and serves only to highlight clearly the concept of *ḥesed*. In this chapter *ḥesed* could be rendered as "covenantal loyalty."

If we read in verse 20 לחסידך for לחסידיך,[55] and, in agreement with Kittel,[56] make it refer to David, it would have to be translated as a "member of your covenanted group."[57] The writer probably alludes to II Sam. 23:1–4.[58] To his elected[59] and anointed Yahweh shows his covenant-based *ḥesed*.[60]

Isa. 55:3,[61] like Ps. 89, goes back to II Sam. 7. In Isa. 55:3 we find almost verbatim the content of Ps. 89:4, 50:

ואכרתה לכם ברית עולם חסדי דוד הנאמנים

Here again we see the relationship between *b^e^rith* and *ḥesed*, as well as the subordination of the latter to the former. חסדי ד' הנ' is here a "closer definition of the object"[62] with regard to *b^e^rith*. Budde translates: "the inviolable mercies of David" and explains, "One might also add the ב of the covenant condition before חסדי. In any event, the sentence must be understood in this way. That which David was promised remains binding and shall find its fulfillment in Israel."[63] Duhm translates "the everlasting mercies of

[55] Cf. Kittel, *Die Psalmen, loc. cit.*; Gunkel, *Die Psalmen* (Göttingen, 1926), *ad. loc.*; König, *Die Psalmen* (Gütersloh, 1926), *ad. loc.*; Duhm, *Die Psalmen* (Tübingen, 1922), *ad. loc.*

[56] Kittel, *loc. cit.*, "It is a 'vision' of David himself, not as in the main narrative of II Sam. 7 of Nathan."

[57] Cf. Isa. 50:5; Cf. ch. II, p. 68.

[58] Kraetzschmar, *op. cit.*, p. 244.

[59] Ps. 89:4.

[60] Cf. Ps. 18:51; II Sam. 22:51; I Sam. 2:10.

[61] II Chron. 6:42.

[62] Delitzsch, Franz, *Biblischer Kommentar über den Propheten Jesaia* (Leipzig, 1879), *ad. loc.*

[63] Budde in *H. S.*[4], *loc. cit.*

David," which should "more closely characterize the covenant . . . What once was promised to David and his house shall come to pass."[64] While these explanations render the correct meaning, the translations are erroneous. This is so, not merely because acts of grace refer to the past and promises to the future,[65] but primarily because חסדי, here determined more specifically by הנאמנים, cannot possibly appear as mercy when connected with *b^erith* in its obligatory manifestation. The only possible translation would be to render *ḥesed* as conduct in accordance with the covenant, or, in this passage, as "covenant" *per se*. We translate, then: "I shall make an alliance with you: the inviolable covenant with David." Translated similarly is זכרה לחסדי דוד עבדך in II Chron. 6:42: "Remember the covenant with David your servant," or, "remember the loyalty sworn to your servant David." The covenantal relationship between Yahweh and David, which corresponded to *ḥesed*, is further emphasized by calling David God's servant.[66]

In I Kings 8:23–25 (II Chron. 6:14–16), in his plea for God's aid, Solomon alludes to the promise concerning David, the *b^erith*, and the corresponding *ḥesed* which Yahweh preserves for those of his servants who walk wholeheartedly before him.[67]

In I Kings 3:6 Solomon says:

> You have shown great *ḥesed* to your servant David, my father, because he dealt with you in loyalty, in righteousness, and in uprightness of heart; and you have kept for him this great *ḥesed*, and have given him a son who sits on his throne this day.

As a result of this promise,[68] Yahweh had acted toward David in accordance with the covenant, just as David had fulfilled the obligations resulting from this *ḥesed* relationship with Yahweh by walking before him in loyalty, righteousness and uprightness. Unexpressed in the above passage remains Solomon's wish, which appears in II Chron. 1:8–9, that Yahweh grant him also the promise given to David: "You have shown great *ḥesed* to my father, and have made me king in his stead. O Yahweh, let your promise to David my father remain unbroken." Solomon refers to Yahweh's *ʾemunah* in praying for the

[64] Duhm, *Das Buch Jesaia* (Göttingen, 1923), *ad. loc.* Similar translations and interpretations appear in the commentaries of Dillmann, Delitzsch, Marti, Haller.

[65] Elbogen, *op. cit.*, p. 44.

[66] Cf. chap. III, pp. 89–91.

[67] *Infra*, chap. III, fn. 156, p. 89.

[68] Cf. II Sam. 7:14–16; Ps. 89; 119:41, 76; Isa. 55:3.

fulfillment of Yahweh's promise to David. In faithfully fulfilling His promise, God should also act toward him according to the demands of covenantal loyalty. That Solomon calls Yahweh's *ḥesed* "great"[69] does not change the characteristic of obligatoriness in the concept *ḥesed*. It is thereby emphasized that it is Yahweh's *ḥesed*, that which he was committed to enact by virtue of his promise.

III. *ḤESED* AS THE RECIPROCAL RELATIONSHIP OF GOD TO HIS PEOPLE

A. God and his Faithful People

In Ps. 85 *ḥesed* occurs as God's conduct in accordance with the covenant toward the people who serve Him faithfully. Those who returned from the Exile had not experienced the fortunate times for which they had hoped.[70] For the people, this could only mean that God had not shown favor in the measure it expected, according to the covenant. For this reason verse 8 pleaded: "Show us your *ḥesed*, O Yahweh, and grant us your salvation." In this verse ישעך is parallel to חסדך. Like *ḥesed*,[71] the salvation of Yahweh, which is included in it,[72] is also granted only to those who fear him.[73] In the prayer itself, there is the assurance of it being heard and the confident faith that a just God will protect and bless the righteous. In verse 9, we read:

> I will hear what God the Lord will speak,[74] God[75] will speak peace[76] to His people, to all the members of His congregation (חסידיו), to those who turn their hearts to Him.[77]

The blissful future is then described in a beautiful vision, in verse 11: "*Ḥesed* and *ᵓemeth* will unite; *ẓedek* and *shalom* will kiss each other." *Ḥesed* has the same meaning here as in verse 8, and together with *ᵓemeth* is a hendiadys and forms an indissoluble unity. The meaning

[69] Cf. remarks on Gen. 19:19, chap. I, p. 43.

[70] Vss. 1–7.

[71] *Infra*, chap. III, fn. 154, p. 89.

[72] *Supra*, chap. I, fn. 29, p. 43.

[73] Vs. 10.

[74] Cf. *B. H.*; Staerk, *loc. cit.*

[75] Staerk, *ibid.*

[76] Cf. König, *loc. cit.*, Bertholet in *H. S.*[4], *ad. loc.*

[77] Cf. *B. H.*; Baethgen, *loc. cit.*; Duhm, *Die Psalmen*, *loc. cit.*; Staerk, *loc. cit.*; Kittel, *loc. cit.*; Bertholet, *loc. cit.*; Gunkel, *loc. cit.*

of *ḥesed* as Yahweh's conduct toward his people, based on the covenant, is emphasized by the parallelism of *ẓedek* and *shalom*. For *ẓedek* is here, as Kautzsch maintains, "the covenantal loyalty, God's loving relationship to Israel, by virtue of the promises made by Him."[78] *Shalom*, in verse 10, seems to be identical with the same word in Isa. 54:10[79] and Jer. 16:5[80] and must also be understood here as Yahweh's conduct toward his people, according to the covenant and the reciprocal relationship existing between them.

A community faithful to God could expect its deliverance from dire need by Yahweh because of his *ḥesed*, his covenant-based conduct through which he renders loyal aid to his people. The prayer in Psalm 44 is to be understood in this sense. The author points to the help once given to the forefathers,[81] by stressing the loyalty that the nation gave toward the covenant.[82] On this he bases his claim to being answered, entreating God in verse 26: "Rise up, come to our help! Deliver us for the sake of thy *ḥesed*."[83]

In Ps. 77 the poet, in the face of his people's plight, is in danger of losing his faith in God's just rule. In deepest despair he asks (vs. 8): "Has His *ḥesed* ceased forever? Is His *ʾemeth* at an end for all time?"[84] The *ḥesed* expected from God on the basis of the covenant, according to which He faithfully assists His people and brings them deliverance, had not materialized. The poet himself supplies the answer concerning his lamentful "why?"[85] God, who had redeemed His people from Egypt and who led them through Moses and Aaron,[86] will certainly intervene once again for His people. God's glory was, so to speak, intertwined with Israel's fate.[87]

Yahweh's *ḥesed* toward his people is repeatedly mentioned in prayers of petition and of thanksgiving in the formula: הודו ליהוה כי טוב כי לעולם חסדו. Only in Ezra 3:11 is Israel explicitly mentioned in the formula. But all the other passages occur only with reference to Israel.[88] Those who fear God sing the psalm of thanksgiving: "His *ḥesed* endures forever,"[89] for God grants His *ḥesed* to those who, by

[78] Kautzsch, *op. cit.*, p. 35.

[79] Cf. chap. III, p. 84.

[80] Cf. chap. III, p. 70.

[81] Vss. 2–9.

[82] Vs. 18.

[83] Ps. 115:1.

[84] Read אמתו instead of אמר. Cf. *B. H.*; Briggs, *loc. cit.*; Duhm, *loc. cit.*; Staerk, *loc. cit.*; Gunkel, *loc. cit.*

[85] Vs. 8.

[86] Cf. vss. 15–16, 21; Exod. 15:13; Ps. 106:45.

[87] Cf. Ps. 115:1; *supra*, pp. 92 f.

[88] Cf. Jer. 33:11; Ps. 100:5; 106:1; 107:1, 8, 15, 21, 31; 118:1–4, 49; 136; I Chron. 16:34, 41; II Chron. 5:13; 7:3; 20:21.

[89] Ps. 118:4.

their fear of the Lord, prove their loyalty to the covenant.[90] The formula occurs in Ps. 106:1; and we read in verse 45: "He remembered for their sake His covenant, and relented[91] according to the abundance of His *ḥesed*."[92] *Ḥesed*, which in this context means conduct in accordance with the covenant,[93] is not to be differentiated from the *ḥesed* in verse 1 nor from the *ḥesed* in all of the other verses where the formula is found. God's goodness, which is mentioned in these passages in connection with His *ḥesed*, in no way influences the established meaning of *ḥesed* and does not lead to a meaning of *ḥesed* as favor, as one might expect. For the pious, it was an act of Yahweh's grace that he had entered into a covenant with them and showed them *ḥesed* in accordance with his promise. His *ḥesed*-deeds were miracles to them.[94] While the *ḥesed* relationship between Yahweh and his people was regarded as having originated through his goodness, *ḥesed* itself remained the mutual relationship of rights and duties which Yahweh had obligated himself to show.[95] In this sense only is *ḥesed* to be understood; for example, Ps. 136:10, at the end of the verse. The reason for Yahweh's smiting the first-born of Egypt (vs. 10), Israel's liberation (vs. 11), casting Pharaoh and his hosts in the Sea of Reeds (vs. 15), slaying mighty kings and otherwise demonstrating all his power for the sake of his people throughout the course of history, must not be sought in his favor, grace or goodness. Yahweh's opposition to the enemies of Israel and his own enemies could not be the result of his grace. He stood by the people of his covenant, faithfully executing the *ḥesed* to which they were entitled by virtue of that relationship. By praising Yahweh at the beginning and at the conclusion of the psalm as the King of kings, the creator of heaven and earth, the sustainer of all living beings, the power he demonstrated in his *ḥesed* for Israel was emphasized anew, and his everlasting *ḥesed* was thereby extolled. *Ḥesed* is best translated in these stereotyped passages as "covenantal loyalty"[96] or "faithful assistance according to the covenant."[97]

[90] Cf. chap. III, p. 89.

[91] Instead of וַיִּנָּחֵם read וַיִּנָּחֵם. Cf. *B. H.*; Exod. 15:13; Ps. 31:4; 45:3; 77:21; Neh. 9:12.

[92] Read חֲסָדוֹ; Cf. *B. H.*; Staerk, Kittel, Bertholet, Gunkel.

[93] Cf. chap. III, pp. 76 f.

[94] Ps. 138:2, 8; 25:10; 119:41, 76; 103:17–18.

[95] Ps. 106:7; 107:8, 15, 21, 31; 136:4; 4:4; 17:7; 31:22.

[96] Ps. 100:5.

[97] Perhaps this meaning of *ḥesed*, as the mighty covenantal aid of Yahweh, is the cause of the confusion of the probably older meaning of *ḥesed* in Ps. 89:9 with

In Ps. 48 we read that, on the occasion of some festival in Jerusalem, the assembled multitude celebrated Yahweh's saving power by which he rescued his people and his city from the conquerors (vss. 5–7). They probably had in mind the threat against Jerusalem by Sennacherib;[98] with grateful hearts they could say: "We recall on your covenantal loyalty, O God, in the midst of your temple" (vs. 10).

In Exod. 15:13[99] *ḥesed* must also be understood as Yahweh's covenantal relationship through which he renders steadfast assistance to his people: "You have led in your *ḥesed* the people whom you have redeemed, you have guided them by your strength to your holy abode." It is significant that here בעזך is parallel to בחסדך; God's might, exercised for the sake of His people, is virtually identical with His *ḥesed*. עז and חסד are not synonymous, but the showing of *ḥesed* can lead to the practice of עז.[100] Here, too, *ḥesed* can be translated as "covenantal loyalty" or "faithfulness according to the covenant." In different contexts *ḥesed* can be translated differently as "faithfulness," "assistance," "covenant," or "love." All these are aspects of the total concept. For example, *ḥesed* is not some kind of arbitrary assistance, but rather that which the members of a covenant are obligated to practice reciprocally. This meaning of *ḥesed* as the faithful, mutual assistance among people who are bound together by a covenantal relationship mirrors, perhaps, the original meaning of the word. Groups were formed so that through reciprocal assistance common dangers could be combated and overall security established. This distinct kind of aid, as well as the whole relationship in accord with the rights and obligations of the community, was called *ḥesed*.

B. God and his People — Loyal Again After its Defection

God practiced *ḥesed* toward His people even after they had turned away from Him through sin, provided that they found Him again through repentance, as evidenced by renewed ethical and religious conviction

---

the Aramaism חסין יה. The latter stands out in the Hebrew construction if it is not, as Briggs, *loc. cit.*, thinks, simply a scribal error. Cf. also Staerk, *loc. cit.* Elbogen, *op. cit.*, p. 46, points out that *ḥesed* in Isa. 40:6 is translated in the Targum by תוקפיה. He then translates *ḥesed* in this context as "confidence." However, cf. Dan. 2:37 where תקפה is synonymous with חסנא.

[98] Cf. Kittel, *loc. cit.*, II Kings 18:17 f.

[99] *Supra*, chap. III, fn. 91.

[100] Concerning the connection between חסד and עז cf. Ps. 59:10–11, 17–18; 62:12–13; 138:2–3.

and conduct. The covenantal relationship between Him and His people could then be reinstated and the people could once again hope to receive His covenant-based *ḥesed*. *Ḥesed* is really the positive element in the pardoning of sins by which God confirms that the union between Him and His people is restored. In this context the translation of *ḥesed* as grace or favor is more justified than elsewhere. To the repentant sinners, even if they have again fulfilled their religious duties with the greatest of zeal and could rightfully hope to receive *ḥesed* from God, His *ḥesed* would still appear to them as grace. In itself, however, *ḥesed* is not grace but faithful love. It is the covenantal loyalty shown by Yahweh even to sinners when they again fulfilled the ordinances of his covenant. In His רחמים and סליחה,[101] God forgives the repentant defectors. In His *ḥesed* He receives them again into His covenant.

I. THE PEOPLE BOUND TO GOD IN MARRIAGE

Hos. 2 reports how Yahweh desires to be reunited in a new marriage pact with Israel after she repents her sin. She was the wife whom he had cast off for her adultery. Just as a marriage in everyday life was based upon the mutual relationship of rights and duties, namely *ḥesed*,[102] so Yahweh wanted to conclude his betrothal with Israel through *ḥesed*. In Hos. 2:21 he mentions the gifts which he intends to bring into the marriage as a kind of purchase price,[103] and in verse 22 he states what he demands of his bride. "I will betroth you to me forever[104] in *ḥesed* and *raḥamim*. I betroth you to me in faithfulness[105] and you shall 'know' Yahweh."[106] Yahweh's covenantal *ḥesed* and *raḥamim* had to be reciprocated by Israel with covenantal loyalty and the recognition of Yahweh. דעת יהוה, which

[101] Kittel, *op. cit.*, p. 402.

[102] Cf. chap. I, pp. 39 f.; p. 60.

[103] It was customary for the groom to pay a certain sum in acquiring a wife. Cf. Gen. 24:53; 31:5; 34:12; II Sam. 3:14.

[104] Nowack, *loc. cit.*; Harper, *loc. cit.*; Sellin, *loc. cit.*; Gressmann, *loc. cit.*, consider וארשתיך לי בצדק ובמשפט res. בצ' ובמ' as a gloss.

[105] Sellin, *loc. cit.*, and Gressmann, *loc. cit.*, connect vs. 22 with Israel. Gressmann alters vs. 22a to read, "I betroth myself to thee." Perhaps it should be read וארשתי לך, "and I am betrothed to thee." Cf. Exod. 22:15; Deut. 22:28. It is impossible to see a reference to Israel's behavior in vs. 21, as Hertzberg does, *op. cit.*, Vol. 40, p. 286. That *ḥesed* as used by Hosea elsewhere depicts a human attitude is no objection. It is impossible for Israel to practice *raḥamim* toward God.

[106] For וידעת read ובדעת. Cf. *B. H.*; Duhm, *Die Zwölf Propheten* (Tübingen, 1910), *ad. loc.*; Nowack, *loc. cit.*; Sellin, *loc. cit.*; Gressmann, *loc. cit.*

is not to be distinguished from דעת אלהים, obligates Israel to practice mutual *ḥesed* and *ᵓemeth* among themselves and toward God.[107] The added expression *raḥamim* does not change the meaning of *ḥesed* as being Yahweh's covenantal relationship toward his people, who are united with him in bonds of matrimony. Yahweh also wants to bring *raḥamim*, which exceeds the bounds of *ḥesed*, into this marriage. If at some future time the people will stray again, Yahweh will not forsake them. If they repent he will, in his mercy, forgive them and keep them. Yahweh will show *raḥamim* as freely as he does *ḥesed*. Ps. 103:13 reads: "As a father pities his children,[108] so Yahweh pities those who fear him." In the same psalm, verses 11, 17, a similar sentiment is expressed in that only those who fear the Lord receive His *ḥesed*.[109] It is but a short step from *ḥesed* to *raḥamim*. *Ḥesed* is covenantal loyalty; *raḥamim* is forgiving love.[110] Yahweh's people had to reciprocate *ḥesed* and *raḥamim* with *ḥesed*. The people, however, could not show *raḥamim* toward Yahweh.

In Isa. 54, Yahweh promises Israel, his bride, who had been chastened by expulsion, to take her back into his favor[111] and forever to show her the *ḥesed* that is entailed in the marriage union. "With everlasting covenantal loyalty I will love you,[112] says Yahweh, your redeemer" (vs. 8). Yahweh bases his relationship with Israel upon a covenant: "For the mountains may depart, and the hills be removed but my loyalty shall not depart from you, and my covenant of peace shall not be removed,[113] says Yahweh, who loves you"[114] (vs. 10). The relatedness of *ḥesed* and *bᵉrith* is again shown here, and *ḥesed* in verse 8 does not mean "mercy" as the close connection with רחמתיך seems to indicate. *Ḥesed*, related to *bᵉrith* and *raḥamim* but not synonymous with either, is the attitude Yahweh shows the members of his covenant. It is to them that he grants his peace.[115]

Jer. 16 states that Yahweh withdraws his peace,[116] which is based upon *ḥesed* and *raḥamim*, from his people which have forsaken

[107] Cf. Hos. 4:6; 6:6; chap. II, pp. 56–58, 61–62.

[108] Maybe רחם should be translated here as "shows himself a kinsman." Cf. Gen. 43:30; I Kings 3:26; Isa. 13:18; 49:15; Jer. 31:20; Amos 1:11.

[109] Cf. chap. III, p. 89.

[110] Cf. Deut. 4:30–31; Jer. 31:3; Ps. 51:3; 103:11–12.

[111] Vs. 7.

[112] Lam. 3:32, 22–23.

[113] Cf. Num. 25:12; Ezek. 34:25; Hag. 2:9; Ps. 85:9, 11; Jer. 20:10; 38:22.

[114] Cf. Deut. 4:30–31, where Yahweh is called אל רחום for keeping the covenant sworn to the patriarchs with those who return to him and obey his commandments.

[115] Ps. 85:9.

[116] Cf. Jer. 11:9 f.; Volz, *Der Prophet Jeremia* to chap. 16:5.

his commandments. Verse 5[117] states: "For so says Yahweh: Do not enter the house of mourning, or go to lament or bemoan them; for I have taken my peace from this people (says Yahweh) my faithfulness and my love."[118] In Jer. 16:5 שלום is the same as ברית שלום in Isa. 54:10, and the phrase אספתי שלום is identical with הפר בריתי.[119] We concur with Giesebrecht and Volz[120] that את החסד ואת הרחמים is not a gloss. But if the latter should be the case, as has occasionally been presumed,[121] then את החסד ואת הרחמים would still constitute a correct explanation[122] of שלומי. They constitute the components of Yahweh's covenant of peace. The judgment meted out to Israel, by the withdrawal of Yahweh's *ḥesed* and *raḥamim*, was harsh. Whoever was condemned to live outside the community, was both outlawed and virtually condemned to death.[123]

In Jer. 3:12–13 Yahweh is described as *ḥasid*. If Israel will return repentant to him, he will not perpetuate his wrath toward faithless Israel,[124] whom he has divorced; perhaps recognizing its sins it will return to him. Because the relationship between Yahweh and Israel was one of a marital union,[125] it is clear that Yahweh, as *ḥasid*, was prepared to show *ḥesed* to his repentant people in accordance with the conduct expected in a matrimonial relationship. As Kraetzschmar correctly states,[126] "the dismissal with a bill of divorce did not preclude compassionate reunion with Israel, but only a temporary expulsion from the land. In good Hoseanic style, divine *ḥesed* is the mediator." *Ḥesed* includes the element of mercy, insofar as Yahweh does not act according to *lex talionis* but is always ready to grant *ḥesed* to those who obey his commandments, even if they had previously strayed from him. For this reason כי חסיד אני, in Jer. 3:12, can be translated as "for I am merciful" or "kind." Yahweh as חסיד is also צדיק. In steadfast reliability,[127] stemming from covenantal obligation, he assists and secures justice for all those who call upon him in loyalty and who fear him.[128]

[117] Jer. 11:1–5.
[118] Volz, *loc. cit.*
[119] Giesebrecht, *loc. cit.*
[120] Cf. Giesebrecht, *ibid.*, Volz, *loc. cit.* Giesebrecht retains the whole phrase נאם יהוה את החסד ואת הרחמים, while Volz strikes נאם יהוה.
[121] Cf. Duhm in *H. S.*[4], *ad. loc.*; Cornill, *Das Buch Jeremia* (Leipzig, 1905), *ad. loc.*; Schmidt, *loc. cit.*
[122] Schmidt, *loc. cit.*
[123] Cf. Volz, *loc. cit.*; chap. I, p. 46.
[124] Vss. 8, 13.
[125] Also vs. 14.
[126] Kraetzschmar, *op. cit.*, pp. 151–2.
[127] Kautzsch, *op. cit.*, pp. 24–5.
[128] Ps. 145:17–20.

2. THE PEOPLE BOUND TO GOD BY CONSANGUINITY

In Jer. 31[129] the relationship between Yahweh and Israel is made analogous to that between father and son.[130] This relationship also entailed God's *ḥesed*.[131] When Ephraim remorsefully does penance, Yahweh turns to him in fatherly compassion.[132] Yahweh could show his *ḥesed* to the people that returned to him. They are like a son to him whom he never ceased to love. "I have loved you with an everlasting love; therefore I have continued my faithfulness to you"[133] (vs. 3). Yahweh demands of his people, with whom he is making a new covenant,[134] that they know him. Knowledge of God on the part of the people means practicing *ḥesed* among themselves and through this, simultaneously, toward God.[135]

In Isa. 63:7–8 Yahweh is praised as the God who grants to his people, his faithful sons, *raḥamim* and *ḥesed* — the mercy which forgives sin and the love which is in accordance with the covenant.[136]

3. THE PEOPLE IN GENERAL IN THE COVENANTAL COMMUNITY

In Ps. 130 the author is conscious of man's sinful nature. Because of it, no man could stand before God were it not for God's forgiveness (סליחה)[137] which is granted to those who obey His moral law. In reliance upon God's promise to His followers,[138] the author admonishes them in verses 7–8: "O Israel, hope in Yahweh! For with Yahweh there is *ḥesed*, and with him is plenteous redemption. He will redeem

[129] Regarding the genuineness of Jer. 31, cf. Volz, *loc. cit.*; Sellin, *Einleitung in das Alte Testament* (Leipzig, 1925), pp. 97–8.

[130] Vss. 9 b–20.

[131] Cf. chap. III, pp. 75 f.

[132] Vss. 18–20.

[133] Cf. Cornill, *loc. cit.*; "משך חסד is connected with the person by ל; we have to assume then in משכתיך the pron. suff. stands for the dative, which presents no grammatical difficulty." Cf. Ps. 36:11; 109:12; Reuss, *loc. cit.*; Volz, *loc. cit.*

[134] Cf. vss. 33–34; Isa. 54:8, 10.

[135] Cf. *supra*, fn. 107, p. 84.

[136] Delitzsch's (*loc. cit.*) explanation of *ḥesed* in Isa. 63:7 as "grace descending upon the sinful creature" is wrong.

[137] Cf. vss. 3–4; Kittel, *loc. cit.*, correctly remarks re Ps. 130:4 that forgiveness is obtained "not by God indiscriminately wiping away sin, out of superficial compassion, but by making His forgiveness dependent upon repentance and the mending of one's ways." (Cf. Jer. 31:34; 33:8.)

[138] Cf. vs. 5; Ps. 119.

Israel from all his iniquities."[139] To those who wait for him,[140] Yahweh grants his covenant and the *ḥesed* corresponding to it. This involves his forgiveness for the sins of the repentant.

In Ps. 90 we have the people's prayer for God's *ḥesed*. Preceding this was the admission of sinfulness (vs. 10) and the desire to achieve an understanding heart (vs. 12). In the hope of obtaining God's forgiveness (vs. 13) the people prayed (vs. 14): "Satisfy us in the morning with your *ḥesed*, that we may rejoice and be glad all our days." They longed for God's *ḥesed* and for communion with Him.

Yahweh is entreated in Num. 14:19: "Pardon the iniquity of this people, according to the greatness of your *ḥesed*." According to the *greatness*[141] of his *ḥesed*, Yahweh could forgive sin. Since the plea for forgiveness was already a sign of repentance and change, it gave to a God, who was in the deepest sense of the covenant a loving God, the possibility of making forgiveness real by granting *ḥesed* to those who had renewed their covenant with Him and whose sins He had forgiven.

The attitude of *ḥesed*, stemming from covenantal obligation following God's forgiveness, closely approaches His favor. Still *ḥesed* is not identical with God's favor. However, since the relationship between God and His people was established by the grace of its election, *ḥesed* is based upon the grace of God. *Ḥesed* characterizes the manner of these relationships which were determined by God, according to the covenant. It could be held that the origin of the God-people (man) relationship stems from God's favor; and that the structuring of these relationships emanates from His ethical will, by which He demands ethical action not only of His elect but, so to speak, of Himself as well. This grace finds its expression in *ḥesed*, His covenant-based conduct.

The *ḥesed*, which occurs in connection with God's grace and the forgiveness of sin, is still different from grace because it is identical with the loyalty characteristic of a group. This is attested to by the fuller expression of the formula in Num. 14:18[142] and in Exod. 34:6 (Ps. 86:15), where the related *ʾemeth* is combined with *ḥesed*.

אל רחום וחנון ארך אפים ורב חסד ואמת.

The phrase in Exod. 34:7, נצר חסד לאלפים, is probably an allusion to the phrase in Exod. 20:6:[143] עשה חסד לאלפים לאוהבי ולשומרי מצותי,

[139] Cf. Bertholet in *H. S.*[4]; König, *loc. cit.*; Staerk, *loc. cit.*

[140] Cf. *infra*, fn. 156, p. 89.

[141] Cf. Ps. 57:11; 86:13; 108:5; 145:8; Gen. 19:19; I Kings 3:6 (II Chron. 1:8).

[142] Cf. Joel 2:18; Jonah 4:2; Ps. 103:8; 145:8; Neh. 9:17.

[143] Cf. Baentsch, *Exodus* (Göttingen, 1903), re Exod. 34:6.

where the conditions revealing the obligatory character of God's *ḥesed* also are clearly shown.[144] As אל רחום וחנון ארך אפים, God forgives the repentant sinner; as אל . . . רב חסד ואמת, He receives into His covenant those who have been forgiven and who again love Him and obey His statutes. His attitude to them corresponds to the demand of loyalty — namely, *ḥesed*. *Ḥesed* may here be translated as "faithful love." In these, as well as other passages, where God's *ḥesed* occurs in connection with His grace, *ḥesed* has a more spiritual meaning. This sublimation consists in the breakthrough of a more or less developed idea, which always occurs in connection with God's *ḥesed* and now appears clearly — namely, that God's *ḥesed*, although understood as being in accordance with the covenant, is viewed not as a right but as a gift. This idea is clarified in Ps. 103 where the psalmist praises God, Who forgives his sins and Who crowns him with *ḥesed* and *raḥamim*, reciprocal love, and forgiving grace.[145]

IV. *ḤESED* AS THE RECIPROCAL RELATIONSHIP OF YAHWEH TO HIS COMMUNITY

A. God and his Faithful

1. GOD AND THOSE WHO KNOW HIM

Yahweh demands of those who wish to obtain his *ḥesed* that they acknowledge him, as is expressed in Jer. 9:23. This means practicing *ḥesed*, *mishpaṭ*, and *ẓedakah*, for Yahweh delights in these.[146] The acceptance of Yahweh is to be understood here in a two-fold sense: one acknowledges Yahweh in his being and actions, and recognizes that the acceptance of Yahweh compels the exercise of *ḥesed*, *mishpaṭ*, and *ẓᵉdakah* by people toward one another and toward God.[147] In Jeremiah, as well as in Hosea, to know Yahweh means to comport oneself in accordance with his ethical commandments.[148] As Cornill

[144] Cf. *infra*, fn. 156, p. 89.

[145] Vs. 4.

[146] In Jer. 9:23 באלה refers to the previously mentioned objects. Cf. Keil, *Biblischer Kommentar über den Propheten Jeremia* (Leipzig, 1872), *ad. loc.*; Hos. 6:6; Mic. 7:18; Ps. 37:28.

[147] Cf. Keil, *loc. cit.*; Orelli, vs., Jeremia, *ad. loc.*; Giesebrecht, *loc. cit.*; Cornill, *loc. cit.*, to Jer. 31:34.

[148] Cf. Jer. 22:15–16; 24:7; 31:34; 2:8; 4:22; 9:2, 5; Hos. 2:22; 4:1; 6:6; 5:4; Ps. 103:6.

rightly remarks,[149] it is in essence identical with what is called ידע את משפט יהוה in Jer. 8:7, and ידע דרך יהוה in Jer. 5:4–5. Knowledge of Yahweh, and action in accordance with the ethical command written by him on the human heart,[150] made communion with him possible. Accordingly, Yahweh was obligated to show his loyal love to those who knew him. The divine *ḥesed*, as the human *ḥesed*, had also to accord with the demands for justice and righteousness.[151] Yahweh loved *ẓedakah* and *mishpaṭ*;[152] his *ḥesed* filled the earth, as Ps. 33:5 stated.[153]

Those who knew God could pray with confidence for His *ḥesed*, as we read in Ps. 36:10: "Continue your *ḥesed* to those who know You, and Your *ẓedakah* to the upright of heart!" *Ẓedakah* is here again parallel to *ḥesed*. In Psalms 119, 149 *mishpaṭ* is parallel to *ḥesed*. *Ẓedakah* and *mishpaṭ* are not synonymous but are contained in *ḥesed* as Yahweh's conduct toward his faithful, in accordance with the covenant.

2. GOD AND THOSE WHO FEAR HIM

While there are a variety of conditions that must be fulfilled by those who wish to be received in God's covenantal community and have a part in His *ḥesed*, they all have the same significance. Those who seek God must prove themselves worthy in order to find Him and be received into His covenant. The fear of God makes the granting of His *ḥesed* possible.[154] As Staerk comments on Ps. 5:8:[155] He who fears God "has recognized Him in His true essence and serves Him strengthened by this blissful knowledge."

Other passages also state that those who love God, serve Him faithfully, keep His commandments and His covenant, and who pray to Him and trust wholly in Him, can confidently expect His *ḥesed*.[156]

[149] Cornill, *loc. cit.*

[150] Jer. 31:33.

[151] Cf. Isa. 16:5; Hos. 12:7; Mic. 6:8; Zech. 7:9; Ps. 101:1; cf. chap. II, pp. 58–59, 61–62. *Supra*, fn. 29, p. 73.

[152] Keil, *loc. cit.*, "*Ḥesed* is the foundation of right and justice."

[153] Cf. Ps. 37:28; 99:4; 103:6; Keil, *ibid.*

[154] Cf. Ps. 5:8; 33:18; 147:11; 103:11, 17; Prov. 16:16; Job 6:14; Ps. 25:10, 14; 31:20; 86:11; 61:6, 8; 85:8 f.; 115:1, 11; 145:17 f.

[155] Staerk, *loc. cit.*

[156] Cf. Exod. 20:6; Deut. 5:10; 7:9; Dan. 9:4; Neh. 1:5; 9:32; Ps. 25:10; 103:17–18; 26:3; 119:159; I Kings 8:23; II Chron. 6:14; Ps. 4:4; 86:5; 145:17–20; Ps. 13:6; 21:8; 32:10; 52:10; 143:8; 17:7; 33:18, 22; 144:2; 147:11.

3. GOD AND HIS SERVANTS

Just as in everyday life *ḥesed* was entailed in the relationship between master and servant,[157] so it characterized the relationship between Yahweh and his servants. If we understand *ḥesed* in this sense, a new light is shed upon the much criticized and unjustly deprecated passage in Ps. 143:12: ובחסדך תצמית איבי והאבדת כל צררי נפשי כי אני עבדך. The usual translation is: "And in your mercy cut off my enemies, and destroy all them that harass my soul, for I am your servant." However much it is recognized that Ps. 143 "is a testimony of great piety and intense desire for salvation,"[158] still the ethical content of the psalm is decried and condemned because of verse 12. This is done most devastatingly and sharply by Duhm, who says:[159]

> By his *mercy* Yahweh is to destroy the enemies of the psalmist! One might almost think that the word originally read בחמתך, "in thy wrath," since mercy in such a context is repulsive. Unfortunately, however, one may expect much of this of the author.

In fact, entreating God's mercy in such a context would appear strange, even if we could put ourselves in the frame of mind of such a fervently naïve worshiper. Several changes have been suggested here for the word *ḥesed* which translated as "mercy" conflicts with the entire ethical and religious content of the preceding verse of this psalm. Gunkel,[160] agreeing with Duhm, suggests בחמתך; Ehrlich (following Gunkel), בחרונך; Perles[161] wants to translate *ḥesed* here as "strength." With great ingenuity, he also suggests the possibility of a metathesis[162] in verses 11–12, so that the original text would read:

בחסדך תוציא מצרה נפשי
ובצדקתך תצמית איבי

All these changes are superfluous if we understand *ḥesed* as conduct corresponding to the covenant by which God helps His faithful.

The worshiper states his relationship to God by calling himself a servant of the Lord, thereby establishing his claim to the fulfillment of his prayer for help against his enemies.[163] The relationship called

[157] Cf. I Sam. 20:8; I Kings 20:31; cf. chap. I, pp. 46; 51–52.
[158] Staerk, *loc. cit.*
[159] Duhm, *loc. cit.*
[160] Gunkel, *loc. cit.*
[161] Perles, *loc. cit.*
[162] *Ibid.*, pp. 114–15.
[163] Cf. Ps. 69:17–18; 86:13, 16; 116:16; 136:22.

forth God's *ḥesed*.[164] Just as God here is to destroy the enemies of His servant because of His *ḥesed*, so He is entreated in Ps. 54:7 to destroy the enemies of His faithful servant in His ᵓ*emeth*. Reference has already been made to the close relationship between *ḥesed* and ᵓ*emeth*.[165] Furthermore, *ḥesed* in Ps. 143, verse 12, is parallel to *ẓ*^{e}*dakah* in verse 11:[166] "... in your righteousness deliver my soul from trouble" — the righteousness by which God does justice to His faithful.[167] God is entreated to destroy His enemies, not because of His mercy but in His *ḥesed*, in accordance with the demands of loyalty and justice — the attitude based on the relationship between Him and His servant. The *ḥesed* might be appropriately translated as "loyalty" or as "loyally given help."

In Ps. 119 an obedient servant of Yahweh,[168] loyal and devoted to him in every respect,[169] entreats for *ḥesed* corresponding to the covenant promised by Yahweh to those members of his community who live in accordance with his will.[170] He clings to God's promise to aid his followers,[171] crying out to God not to let him sink before his enemies, but in His *ḥesed* to keep him alive in accordance with the covenantal agreement.[172] With remarkable confidence in the fulfillment of God's promise of *ḥesed*, he says in verse 160:[173] "When I reckon, the sum of your word is truth; and every one of your righteous ordinances endures for ever."[174] *Ḥesed* is parallel to תשועתך in verse 41; in verse 149 it is parallel to כמשפטיך. Verse 40 reads בצדקתך חיני instead of כחסדך חיני. *Ḥesed* is to be understood here only as conduct in accordance with the covenant promised by Yahweh in his faithfulness, whereby in his justice and righteousness he grants aid to his faithful servants. Their concern was not merely to be kept alive through God's *ḥesed*, but to give their lives meaning and purpose through the *ḥesed* rooted in the covenantal relationship. This is also the meaning of *ḥesed* in Ps. 31:17: "Let your face shine on your servant; save me by your loyal covenantal love."

[164] Cf. *supra*, chap. III, fn. 157.

[165] Cf. Ps. 57:4; *supra*, chap. III, fn. 15, p. 72.

[166] Cf. vs. 1; Ps. 5:9.

[167] Kautzsch, *op. cit.*, p. 47.

[168] Cf. vss. 76, 124, 122, 125, 140.

[169] Cf. vss. 8, 34–35, 42–63, 94 f.

[170] Cf. vss. 41, 76; Ps. 138:2.

[171] Cf. vss. 25, 28, 38, 42, 49, 58, 65, 74, 81–82, 107, 114, 116, 123, 133, 140, 148, 154, 169–170.

[172] Cf. vss. 88, 149, 159, 40; in vs. 149 כחסדך and כמשפטך are probably to be exchanged. Cf. *B. H.*

[173] Vs. 89.

[174] Cf. Delitzsch, *loc. cit.*; Staerk, *loc. cit.*

4. GOD'S FAITHFUL IN A GENERAL SENSE

a. *The prayer for the granting of God's ḥesed*

The longing for God's *ḥesed* by the pious is not to be explained by their understandable wish to be delivered out of their straits but, foremost, because deliverance through *ḥesed* would give them assurance of being in a covenantal relationship with God. They believed in His *ḥesed* even when their actual fate sometimes brought them close to despair. For them, the most precious thing in life, and an end in itself, was the covenantal relationship to God which was manifested by *ḥesed*. With the profound intuition of the truly pious, they felt and knew that God was willing to accept into a covenantal relationship those who returned to Him. By their favorable conduct before God they bore witness to His ethical and religious plan. Even more than they were seeking Him did God wish that they would find Him so that He could show them His covenantal *ḥesed*.[175] When they were conscious of their real worthiness and prayed to God for deliverance from their troubles and the preservation of their lives, they were already basically convinced that God would take their part and show them *ḥesed* for the sake of His covenant with them, of which *ḥesed* was the primary expression. John Hempel writes:

> Israel shares the oriental horror of death. However, it liberates itself from this not by myth but by the individual's hard-won belief in Yahweh's power and the deep conviction that it is not only the creature that desires communion with the creator, but that the creator also desires communion with his creature.[176]

In Ps. 6:5 a pious man, under attack by evildoers and enemies, prays:[177] "Turn to me Yahweh, save my life; deliver me for the sake of your *ḥesed*."[178] The appeal to Yahweh to deliver his faithful for the sake of his *ḥesed*[179] is almost a test for him. It is impossible for Yahweh to permit his faithful to succumb to their enemies, who are likewise his enemies; his cause is bound up with that of his

[175] Cf. Mic. 7:18; Jer. 9:23.

[176] Joh. Hempel in his review of Quell, *Die Auffassung des Todes in Israel* (Leipzig, 1925), in *Theol. Literaturzeitung*, 1926, No. 6, p. 125.

[177] Vss. 8–11.

[178] Cf. Briggs, *loc. cit.*; Duhm, *Die Psalmen, ad. loc.*; König, *loc. cit.*; Bertholet *loc. cit.*

[179] Cf. Ps. 44:27; 115:1; cf. chap. III, p. 79.

faithful. Therefore, the worshiper emphasizes in verse 6: "For in death there is no remembrance of you; in Sheol who praises you?" Similarly in Ps. 88 a true servant of the Lord, hopelessly ill with leprosy from which he has suffered from his youth, believing himself near death,[180] feels that God has rejected him.[181] Verses 12–13 read: "Is your *ḥesed* declared in the grave, or your *ʾemunah* in *ʾAvaddon*? Are your wonders known in the darkness, or your righteousness in the land of forgetfulness?" Underlying the "why" of the psalm is, as Staerk remarks, "the faith that will not and cannot give up God."[182] Also in Ps. 6 the worshiper is sure of divine aid, the evildoers will be disgraced and the covenant with God will thus be confirmed.[183]

The pious thought of death as horror,[184] since they believed that all relationships between men and God ceased in Sheol. They could no longer enjoy the *ḥesed* God granted them according to the covenant. Without *ḥesed* life was without meaning to them. "Your *ḥesed* is indeed better than life!" exclaims the psalmist (Ps. 63:3).[185] Here חסדך can indeed be translated as "communion with you." Their ideal was to receive חיים and חסד from God, as expressed in Job 10:12: "You gave me life and have dealt loyally with me; your care has preserved my breath."[186]

God's faithful, who by a just and moral life had an ethical relationship with Him, could expect salvation through *ḥesed* from a true and just God, for the sake of His *ḥesed*. In Ps. 109:26 (cf. vs. 21) the prayer is uttered: "Help me, Yahweh my God! Save me according to your loyal love!" The worshiper knew himself to be a just man, one who practiced *ḥesed* toward his fellow men and, therefore, also toward God.[187] This was in contrast to his oppressor who had not even shown *ḥesed* to the poor.[188] For this reason he could pray so fervently to God not to grant *ḥesed* to his adversary[189] but, in accordance with the covenant, to grant it to himself.

In Ps. 43:1 God is entreated by a pious man to protect him from

[180] Cf. vss. 15, 16; Staerk, *loc. cit.*; Kittel, *loc. cit., passim.*

[181] Vs. 15.

[182] Staerk, *loc. cit.*

[183] Vss. 9–11.

[184] Cf. Ps. 13:4–6; Job 13:14; *supra*, fn. 21, p. 41; cf. Ps. 39, 49, 73, 90.

[185] Cf. Staerk, *loc. cit.*; Ps. 73:25; 36:8 f.; 94:16 f.; cf. chap. III, pp. 95 ff.

[186] After חיים read with Budde (*Das Buch Hiob* [Göttingen, 1913], *ad. loc.*) s.v. נחת לי; cf. Prov. 21:21; Ps. 119:88, 149, 159.

[187] Vss. 4–5.

[188] Vs. 12.

[189] Vs. 16; cf. chap. II, p. 62.

his oppressors and grant him justice; otherwise[190] he would feel himself expelled from God's communion. "Vindicate me, Yahweh, and defend my cause against those who do not belong to your community (מגוי לא חסיד), from deceitful and unjust men deliver me!" Verse 1b explains the phrase מגוי לא חסיד in full and explains why those who are so designated could not be members of God's covenantal community. In Ps. 43, which is the continuation of Ps. 42,[191] the pious man, whose sole desire is to be allowed to dwell in the presence of the Lord,[192] prays to God to deliver him from his plight. It seems to him that his enemies are justified if they mock him with the question, "Where is your God who should have helped you?"[193] So he entreats God in verse 9 to grant him His *ḥesed*.[194] He longs for the exercise of God's covenantal loyalty, whereby God brings help to His faithful — not only for the sake of the assistance but, above all, in order to attain the certainty of participation in God's covenant. His prayer expresses his assurance of God's salvation.[195] The phrase יצוה יהוה חסדו becomes intelligible on the basis of the recognition that *ḥesed* is personified in the religious symbolism of the worshiper. God's *ḥesed* is like a messenger sent to assist His faithful. *Ḥesed* and *ᵓemeth* are as angels which God sends from heaven to carry out His divine will on earth together with the members of His covenant.[196] Made analogous to people, *ḥesed* and *ᵓemeth* meet, *ẓedek* and *shalom* kiss each other.[197] The pious conceived of *ḥesed* which they considered the highest good, in still another way. God's *ḥesed* was viewed as being not only mighty and great[198] but as filling the whole world,[199] reaching to the very heavens.[200] Is there any better proof for the importance of the concept of *ḥesed* in biblical thought than that in mystical contemplation it becomes personified?

Conscious of having done religious works for the city of God and the worship of God, Nehemiah asks that God be gracious to him in accordance with the fullness of His *ḥesed*, as Nehemiah had done

[190] Vs. 2.

[191] Cf. Staerk, Kittel, Gunkel, König, *et al.*

[192] Vss. 2–3.

[193] Cf. vss. 4, 10–12.

[194] Vs. 9 is mixed up. With Kittel, *loc. cit.*; Bertholet, *loc. cit.*, יצוה is to be considered as a jussive.

[195] Cf. vss. 6, 12, 43:5.

[196] Cf. Ps. 57:4; 40:12; 61:8; Prov. 20:28; Ps. 23:6; 89:15; 59:11; 85:11–14; 43:3; Briggs, *op. cit.*, re Ps. 57:4; Kessler, *op. cit.*, re Ps. 23:6.

[197] Ps. 85:11.

[198] Cf. Ps. 86:13; 145:8; Num. 14:19; Briggs, *op. cit.*, re Ps. 86:13.

[199] Cf. Ps. 33:5; 119:64.

[200] Cf. Ps. 57:11; 108:5; 36:6; 103:11.

(Neh. 13:22). In vs. 14 he applies the term חסדי[201] to his pious deeds, which have proved his devotion to God. Reverentially he asks for God's loyalty, which God shows to the members of His covenant. The formulation of his prayer, וחוסה עלי כרב חסדך, expresses not only the deep religiosity and reverence of Nehemiah toward God, but also the understanding that the covenant, and the corresponding *ḥesed* which God grants to His faithful, emanates ultimately from his mercy.

b. *The confident faith in God's granting of ḥesed*

In Ps. 23:6 we read: "Surely טוב וחסד shall follow me all the days of my life; and I shall 'abide' in the house of the Lord for ever."[202] In the certainty of covenantal relationship with God, the pious person is not afraid of life. God is his guide and host. He may abide in His house, and there he is sheltered. Just as a guest may expect *ḥesed*, loyalty, from his host,[203] so he whose soul is in intimate communion with God is certain of receiving *ḥesed* in God's household.[204] To him, for whom communion with God is the greatest good, God's *ḥesed*, His love for His followers, is comparable to God's טוב, His goodness.[205]

To this quiet confidence is added the trust in God's *ḥesed*, obtained through the most difficult inner struggles and caused by the direst trouble, as depicted in Ps. 13:5: "But I have trusted in your steadfast love,[206] my heart shall rejoice in your salvation.[207] I will sing to the

[201] Cf. II Chron. 32:32; 35:26. It is noteworthy that what is called גבורתו in II Kings 20:20 (cf. I Kings 16:27; 22:46; II Kings 10:34; 13:8, 12; 14:15) is called חסדיו 'in II Chron. 32:32 (35:26). It appears that the Chronicler made the change not only to get an edifying effect but because גבורה in a sense is actually identical with חסד. Just as in a secular group the members had to come to each other's assistance and sometimes had to fight for one another with all their power and strength, so the faithful in their acts of *ḥesed* had to employ all their might for God's cause. Perhaps the original meaning was such an act of loyal assistance and its meaning as behavior in accordance with the mutually-obligatory relationship among allies stemmed from that origin. The Chronicler did not choose "the ambiguous word in order to hint that the 'strength' of the two kings lay in their piety," as Perles says (*op. cit.*, p. 89). He called the mighty and powerful deeds of Hezekiah and Josiah *ḥesed*-deeds because they served, in his opinion, to strengthen God's covenant community. In a similar sense the deeds of Nehemiah were *ḥesed*-deeds.

[202] Read וישבתי instead of ושבתי. Cf. *B. H.*; Staerk, Gunkel, Duhm, König, Kittel.

[203] Cf. chap. I, pp. 43 f.

[204] Cf. Ps. 5:8; 48:10; 52:10.

[205] Cf. Ps. 31:20; טוב וחסד are nowhere else paired, as Delitzsch remarks, *Die Psalmen* (Leipzig, 1894), *ad. loc.*

[206] König, *loc. cit.*, translates חסד as "loyalty."

[207] Cf. *supra*, fn. 29, p. 73.

Lord, because he has dealt bountifully with me." Consequently, the psalmist himself provides an answer to his plaintive "why" when oppressed by the godless. God will grant him *ḥesed* and, in mutual loyalty according to the covenant, will stand by him and render him aid.

Ps. 21:8 states that the king who trusts in Yahweh can be sure that, because of God's *ḥesed,* he will not waver. Here, confidence is expressed that he who fulfills the conditions of the divine covenant, who trusts in God alone and puts his hope in Him, will receive God's *ḥesed* and may expect His help.[208]

The faithful one, in life's darkest moments, derives encouragement from the confidence that he will not be deprived of God's *ḥesed.* Thus it states in Ps. 94:17–18: "If Yahweh had not been my help, my soul would soon have dwelt in the land of silence.[209] When I thought, My foot slips, your *ḥesed,*[210] Yahweh, held me up."[211] As in Ps. 21:8, *ḥesed* is not grace but a condition of mutuality, according to which Yahweh reciprocally renders his loyal aid to his faithful. This is how the relationship of חסד in vs. 18 to עזרתה in vs. 17[212] is to be understood, as well as the fact that God, who saves by His *ḥesed,* is called the fortress of the pious, the rock of his refuge (vs. 22). In this context *ḥesed* could be rendered correctly as "covenantal loyalty" or "loyal aid reciprocated."

In Ps. 59, in the midst of great distress, a religious man proclaims his confidence that he will receive *ḥesed* from God. We read in verses 9–10: "O my strength, I will sing praises to you; for God is my fortress. My God — His *ḥesed* will meet me, God will let me look in triumph on my enemies."[213] Verses 17–18 are almost identical:

> But I will sing of your might; I will rejoice in your *ḥesed* every morning for you are a fortress to me and a refuge in the day of my distress.
>
> O my strength, I will sing to you, for you, God, are my fortress, my God — his *ḥesed* greets me. God will let me look in triumph over my enemies.[214]

Perles[215] sees in these verses the meaning of "strength" in *ḥesed* and points to the close connection between חסד and משגב to support his

[208] Prov. 10:30.

[209] Cf. chap. III, pp. 92 f.

[210] Cf. Ps. 3:6; 18:36; 38:17; Briggs, *loc. cit.*

[211] Cf. Staerk, *loc. cit.*, Bertholet in *H. S.*[4], *ad. loc.*

[212] Cf. Ps. 44:27; 109:26.

[213] Cf. *B. H.*; Duhm, Staerk, Kittel, König, Gunkel, Bertholet.

[214] Cf. *B. H.*; Staerk, Kittel.

[215] Perles, *op. cit.*, p. 89.

contention. With the same justification he might have pointed to the parallel עז. The fact that חסד is used parallel to or beside משגב or עז or some similar term does not prove that it means "strength." Perles' suggestion is justified only insofar as the meaning "strength" is contained in the overall concept of *ḥesed*. It is through his *ḥesed*, through his conduct based on the covenant, that Yahweh exercises his strength and saving power (עז)[216] for his faithful and becomes for them a fortress and a refuge. Here, as in Ps. 144:2, where Perles again proposes "strength" as the translation of *ḥesed*, *ḥesed* can only be understood as Yahweh's conduct toward his faithful, based on the covenant. The correct translation, therefore, is "faithfulness, loyalty according to the covenant" or "help, loyally given as promised in the covenant." All suggested changes are therefore superfluous.[217]

This also throws some light on the much disputed passage, Jonah 2:8: "Those[218] who honor vain idols forsake their *ḥesed*." As Sellin[219] says, *ḥesed* is here a metonym for God. Those who do not serve God alone, with all their hearts, deprive themselves of the source of their only true salvation. They are bound to lose that covenantal relationship with God, according to which He loyally aids His followers by showing them reciprocal *ḥesed*. In this context *ḥesed* may well be rendered as "their covenant with God" or perhaps "their loyal assistance." It is absolutely unnecessary to read מחסיהם for חסדם.[220] That this interpretation of *ḥesed* is correct is proven by the reverse picture in Ps. 31:7–8. He who hates the worthless idols and trusts in God alone enjoys God's loyal *ḥesed*, corresponding to the covenant, and finds deliverance from all distress.

The word חסדו in Isa. 40:6 could perhaps also be rendered as "aid" or "support" or "might." However, it is probable that we read חסנו instead of חסדו, as does Marti.[221]

In Job 37:13 חסד is the opposite of שבט, "scourge," and must be understood as Yahweh's loyal love for his faithful, or, more precisely, as "loyal aid rendered according to the covenant." The

[216] Cf. Isa. 26:1; 49:5; Jer. 16:19; Ps. 28:7; *passim*.

[217] It has been suggested to read for חסד . . . חסני, סלעי, חזקי, מחסי. Cf. *B. H.*, Gunkel, Bertholet, Duhm, Staerk, Ehrlich (after Gunkel) *et al.*

[218] For משמרים read השמרים; cf. *B. H.*; Nowack, *Die Kleinen Propheten*, *ad. loc.*; Marti, *Das Dodekapropheton* (Tübingen, 1904), *ad. loc.*; Sellin, *Das Zwölfprophetenbuch*, *ad. loc.*; Ps. 31:7.

[219] Sellin, *loc. cit.*

[220] Cf. Marti, *loc. cit.*; *B. H.*

[221] Cf. Marti, *Das Buch Jesaia* (Tübingen, 1900), *ad. loc.*; Perles, *op. cit.*, thinks that here, too, *ḥesed* has the meaning of "strength."

same contrast between שבט and חסד is found in Ps. 89:33–34 and in II Sam. 7:14–15.

In Ps. 62 a religious man's conviction is expressed — that God, the just ruler, will deal with His faithful according to *ḥesed*. He says in verses 12–13:[222] "God has spoken once, twofold have I heard it: that power belongs to God; and that to you, O Lord, belongs *ḥesed*. For you requite a man according to his doing." *Ḥesed* is here not parallel to,[223] but in contrast with, עֹז, for עֹז represents God's punishing powers.[224] The religious man had learned two great truths:[225] God makes His adversaries feel His punishing power; but He accepts into His communion those who, conscious of the vanity of all human life and worldly wealth,[226] trust in Him alone, and accordingly grants them *ḥesed*. God is for them a safe refuge and a firm support.[227] Concerning verses 11–12, Delitzsch[228] remarks:

> Everybody is repaid according to his actions, which express his relationship to God. He who rises against God's will and order feels God's עֹז, His crushing punishing power, and he who is desirous of salvation submits to God's will, receives *ḥesed* from God. *Ḥesed* is the promised reward of faithfulness out of God's great abundance — his submission brings him life, and his confidence becomes surety.

The pious clung to God with unshakable confidence; and they praised Him with thankful hearts for *ḥesed*, either already granted or in certainty expected.[229] Through *ḥesed*, the most valuable good of all was characterized, namely — the covenantal relationship with God.

B. God and Those Who Become Loyal to Him Again After Their Defection

"Have mercy on me, O God, according to your *ḥesed*; according to your abundant *raḥamim* blot out my transgressions." This is how the supplicant in Ps. 51:1 approaches God in the knowledge that God demands of His faithful the sacrifices of righteousness, of the contrite

[222] Ps. 89:36.
[223] *Supra*, chap. III, fn. 100, p. 82.
[224] Ps. 89:11.
[225] Cf. Delitzsch, *loc. cit.*
[226] Vss. 10–11.
[227] Cf. vss. 2–3, 8–9.
[228] Cf. Delitzsch, *loc. cit.*; Duhm, *loc. cit.*
[229] Cf. also Ps. 31:8, 22; 66:20; 4:4; 57:4, 11; 86:13; Isa. 63:7; Ps. 107:43; Hos. 14:10; Ps. 37:25, 28; I Sam. 2:4–10; Ps. 146:6 f.; 106:7; 36:6, 8; 92:2–3.

heart and humble spirit.[230] In His forgiving grace, God could blot out his sins and show him loving *ḥesed*, according to the covenant.

In Mic. 7:18 it is expressed that God pardons sins, does not keep His wrath forever and willingly shows *ḥesed*, but only to those who (this is not spelled out here), in Mic. 6:8, do justice, are merciful and humble before God.[231] In Ps. 86:5 this is explicitly stated: "For you, O Lord, are good, forgiving, and loving to all who call on you." That *ḥesed* in Mic. 7:18 does not objectively signify "favor" or "grace" is confirmed also in Mic. 7:20, where *ḥesed* is parallel to *ʾemeth*.[232]

In Lam. 3:31–32 we read: "For the Lord will not cast off for ever, but, though He cause grief, He will have compassion according to the abundance of His *ḥesed*." From those who have forsaken Him, He demands true repentance and renewed loyalty.[233] Then they will again be worthy of His everlasting *raḥamim* and *ḥesed*, which He loyally shows His faithful.[234]

In Ps. 25 a man of faith prays for God's *ḥesed* in the knowledge that God grants His *ḥesed* and *ʾemeth* only to those who keep His covenant and His testimonies.[235] He openly admits his past transgressions but knows himself to be a true servant of God.[236] In verses 6–7 he prays: "Be mindful of your mercy, O Jahweh, and of your *ḥesed*-deeds, for they have been from eternity. The sins of my youth, remember not; according to your *ḥesed* remember mine."[237] He asks God in His mercy to forgive him for the sins of his youth; and in admitting him again into His covenant, to deal with him accordingly. In verses 6–7 through verse 25 *ḥesed* is distinctly defined in this manner. Yahweh, in his loyalty, acts accordingly with those who keep his covenant.

Ps. 40:10–11 indicates clearly that *ḥesed*, though related to *raḥamim*, is not quite synonymous with it and ought not be understood as mercy. Here, *ḥesed* is again connected with the explanatory *ʾemeth*, which is not characteristic of *raḥamim*. Trusting that Yahweh will receive his faithful back[238] into his communion even if they have sinned against him,[239] the worshiper prays for his *raḥamim*, *ḥesed* and *ʾemeth*.

[230] Vss. 18–21.
[231] Cf. chap. II, pp. 71, 73.
[232] Cf. chap. III, p. 73 f.
[233] Vss. 40–42.
[234] Vss. 22–23.
[235] Vs. 25.
[236] Vss. 2–6.
[237] Cf. Staerk, *loc. cit.*; Kittel, *loc. cit.*
[238] Vss. 8–10.
[239] Vs. 13.

> Your righteousness[240] I have sealed in my heart. I have spoken of your faithfulness and salvation; your *ḥesed* and *ᵓemeth* I have not concealed from the great assembly. Similarly may you O Yahweh not seal off your *raḥamim* from me, may your *ḥesed* and *ᵓemeth* protect me.[241]

Even if verse 10 is not completely in order,[242] it is still significant that *ẓᵉdakah*, *ᵓemunah* and *tᵉshuah*, occur before *ḥesed* and *ᵓemeth*. They are contained in *ḥesed* and *ᵓemeth*,[243] which, Delitzsch[244] remarks, "are the alpha and omega of the qualities through which God manifests himself and which lead to salvation." As is true in general, in this psalm also the devout have learned that even when God deals according to the covenant with his *ḥasidim*,[245] the divine intention in itself is still an act of grace, especially if those who seek God are those who have once forsaken him. Thus the religious man prays for proof of *raḥamim* and then for God's *ḥesed* and *ᵓemeth*.

In Ps. 69 a man of faith asks for deliverance from his distress.[246] He confesses that he is a transgressor,[247] but one who now puts his hope in God alone. Taking God's part had brought him trouble.[248] Having devoted himself entirely to God,[249] he may expect that God will deal with him according to the covenant. In his deep piety he prays: "In the abundance of your covenantal love, Yahweh, answer me with your loyal help."[250] He adds in verse 16: "Answer me, Yahweh, after the goodness[251] of your love, according to your abundant mercy, turn to me." In verse 17, as in verse 14, *ḥesed* must be regarded as conditioned by *ᵓemeth*. For the pious, all that God did was full of love and grace.

[240] Ps. 5:9.

[241] Cf. König, *loc. cit.*; Kittel, *loc. cit.*

[242] Cf. Duhm, Staerk, Gunkel; however, Delitzsch, Kittel, Bertholet, König leave the text unaltered.

[243] *Supra*, chap. III, fn. 29, p. 73.

[244] Delitzsch, *loc. cit.*

[245] Cf. chap. II, p. 67.

[246] Vs. 5.

[247] Vs. 6.

[248] Vss. 7–8.

[249] Vs. 9; Deut. 33:9.

[250] Staerk, *loc. cit.*, *passim.*

[251] Read כְּטוּב instead of כִּי־טוֹב. Cf. *B. H.*; Briggs, Gunkel, *et al.*

V. *ḤESED* AS THE RECIPROCAL RELATIONSHIP OF GOD AND MANKIND TO HIS COMMUNITY

The passages treated so far show *ḥesed* as Yahweh's direct action toward his faithful. Now we have to consider several passages in which God's *ḥesed* consists of divinely ordered conduct of others toward His faithful.

Gen. 39:21 reads: "Yahweh was with Joseph and showed him *ḥesed*[252] in that he gave him favor in the sight of the prison keeper." The special relationships between Yahweh and Joseph are characterized by the words ויהי יהוה את יוסף. Because Yahweh was with Joseph, Joseph succeeded in everything he did.[253] Yahweh's covenant-based conduct corresponded to this relationship insofar as he gained the warden's favor for Joseph. Several commentators suggest וַיַּט אליו חסד instead of וַיֵּט אליו חסד, making reference to Ezra 7:28, 9:9, meaning "he let him gain *ḥesed*." This is possible and it would then signify that Yahweh acted toward Joseph in accordance with *ḥesed* in making the prison keeper treat Joseph according to *ḥesed*, to wit — treat Joseph as if there were a covenantal relationship between them.[254] However, as Ball[255] pointed out, if one looks at Isa. 66:12, וַיֵּט could be correct.[256]

Ezra 7:28 and 9:9 mention the *ḥesed* which the Jews had received from the Persians during Ezra's time. They had been permitted to return to Jerusalem and had even been granted public funds for the restoration of the Temple. The Jews, then, had been treated in a manner appropriate for loyal subjects, namely — with *ḥesed*, as had been done in former times by a king of Israel.[257] But Ezra and the rest of the Jews clearly understood that His *ḥesed* was not voluntarily shown them by the Persians. It was induced by God. Ezra 7:27–28 reads:

> Blessed be Yahweh, the God of our fathers, who put such a thing as this into the heart of the king, to beautify Yahweh's

[252] Cf. Reuss, *loc. cit.*; Procksch, *loc. cit.*

[253] Cf. vss. 2–3, 23.

[254] Cf. *supra*, chap. I, fn. 13, p. 39.

[255] Ball, *The Book of Genesis* (Leipzig, 1896), *ad. loc.*

[256] Ehrlich, *op. cit.*, Vol. I (Leipzig, 1896): "As an object to וַיֵּט, if this is the correct text, rather than read וַיֵּט, חסד can only be understood as referring to JHVH himself and would mean: and he was gracious towards him: for to let somebody win the favor of another is הטה חסד."

[257] Cf. I Kings 20:31; cf. chap. I, p. 41.

> house in Jerusalem and to me he extended the *ḥesed* of the king and his counselors, and all the king's mighty officers. I took courage, for the hand of Yahweh was upon me, and I gathered leading men from Israel to go up with me.

Yahweh, "the God of our fathers" as Ezra calls him, in order to emphasize the close relationship between Yahweh and the Jews, has shown them the *ḥesed* which is in accordance with this relationship, by inducing the Persians to deal with them in the spirit of covenantal loyalty.

Similarly, *ḥesed* is to be understood in this manner in Dan. 1:9: "And God gave Daniel favor and compassion in the sight of the lord high chamberlain."

Summary

We may now draw the following conclusions:

A. God's *ḥesed* can only be understood as Yahweh's covenantal relationship toward his followers.

B. If God's *ḥesed* is comprehended in this manner, then it is certain that only those who stand in an ethical and religious relationship to Him may receive and expect His *ḥesed*.

C. God's *ḥesed* corresponds to the demands of loyalty, justice and righteousness and already contains these concepts. God's *ḥesed* and ᵓ*emeth* are to be considered a hendiadys, in which ᵓ*emeth* has the value of a descriptive adjective.

D. In His *ḥesed* God manifests His strength and power in behalf of His faithful and brings them aid and salvation.

E. God's *ḥesed* is the result of His covenant, or His promise or oath.

F. The *ḥesed* of God is very closely related to His *raḥamim* but distinguished from it by its more positive character. The characteristic of loyalty which belongs to the concept of *ḥesed* is alien to the concept of *raḥamim*.

G. The *ḥesed* of God, while it is not to be identified with His grace, is still based upon the latter, insofar as the relationship between God and people, structured by Him as a covenantal relationship, was effected by electing Israel through an act of grace.

H. The significance of *ḥesed* can be rendered by "loyalty," "mutual aid" or "reciprocal love."

Bibliography

Baentsch, B. *Exodus, Leviticus, Numeri.* (Göttingen, 1903). H.K.

Baethgen, F. *Die Psalmen.* (Göttingen, 1904). H.K.

Ball, C. J. *The Book of Genesis.* (Leipzig, 1896). S.B.O.T.

Beer, G. *Der Text des Buches Hiob.* (Marburg, 1897).

Benzinger, I. *Hebräische Archäologie.* (Tübingen, 1907).

Bertheau, E. *Das Buch der Richter und Ruth.* (Leipzig, 1883). E.H.

Briggs, C. A. *A Critical and Exegetical Commentary on The Book of Psalms.* (Edinburgh, 1916). I.C.C.

Brugsch, M. *Arabisch-Deutsches Handwörterbuch.* (Hannover, 1924).

Budde, K. *Das Buch Hiob.* (Göttingen, 1913). H.K.

———. *Die Bücher Samuel.* (Tübingen und Leipzig, 1902). H.C.

———. *Die Religion des Volkes Israel bis zur Verbannung.* (Giessen, 1900).

Cheyne, T. K. in *Encyclopaedia Biblica*, p. 2826. (London, 1899).

Cornill, C. H. *Das Buch Jeremia.* (Leipzig, 1905).

Dalman, G. *Die richterliche Gerechtigkeit im Alten Testament.* (Berlin, 1897).

Delitzsch, Franz. *Biblischer Kommentar über den Propheten Jesaia.* (Leipzig, 1879). B.C.

———. *Biblischer Kommentar über die Psalmen*, hersg. von Friedrich Delitzsch. (Leipzig, 1894). B.C.

———. *Das Salomonische Spruchbuch.* (Leipzig, 1873). B.C.

Dillmann, A. *Der Prophet Jesaia.* (Leipzig, 1890). E.H.

Doughty, C. M. *Wanderings in Arabia.* (London, 1908).

Driver, S. R. *A Critical and Exegetical Commentary on Deuteronomy.* (Edinburgh, 1912).

———. *Notes on the Hebrew Text of the Books of Samuel.* (Oxford, 1890).

Duhm, B. *Das Buch Jesaia.* (Göttingen, 1923). H.K.

———. *Das Buch Jeremia.* (Tübingen, 1901). H.C.

———. *Die Psalmen.* (Tübingen, 1922). H.C.

———. *Die Zwölf Propheten.* (Tübingen, 1910). H.K.

Ehrlich, A. B. *Randglossen zur Hebräischen Bibel.* Vol. III. (Leipzig, 1910).

Elbogen, I. "חסד-Verpflichtung, Verheissung, Bekräftigung" in *Festschrift für Paul Haupt.* (Leipzig, 1926).

———. *Der jüdische Gottesdienst in seiner geschichtlichen Entwicklung.* (Leipzig, 1924).

Frankenberg, W. *Die Sprüche.* (Göttingen, 1898). H.K.

Giesebrecht, F. *Das Buch Jeremia.* (Göttingen, 1907). H.K.

Gressmann, H. *Die älteste Geschichtsschreibung und Prophetie Israels*². (Göttingen, 1921). A.S.

———. *Die Anfänge Israels*². (Göttingen, 1922). A.S.

Gunkel, H. *Genesis.* (Göttingen, 1910).

———. *Die Psalmen.* (Göttingen, 1926). H.K.

———. *Die Urgeschichte und die Patriarchen*². (Göttingen, 1921). A.S.

Haupt, P. *American Journal of Semitic Languages and Literatures*, Vol. XXVI.

Harper, W. R. *A Critical and Exegetical Commentary on Amos and Hosea.* (Edinburgh, 1910).

Hertzberg, H. W. *Die Entwicklung des Begriffes* משפט *im Alten Test.* ZAW, 1922.

Hoffmann, J. *Hiob.* (Kiel, 1891).

Kautzsch, E. *Die Heilige Schrift*³,⁴. (Tübingen, 1909, 1922).

———. *Über die Derivate des Stammes* צדק *im Alttestamentl. Sprachgebrauch.* (Tübingen, 1881).

Keil, C. F. *Biblischer Kommentar über den Propheten Jeremia.* (Leipzig, 1872). B.C.

Kessler, H. *Die Psalmen.* (München, 1899). K.K.

Kittel, R. *Biblia Hebraica.* (Leipzig, 1913).

———. *Geschichte des Volkes Israel.* (Stuttgart Gotha, 1923, 5).

———. *Die Psalmen*³·⁴. (Leipzig, 1922). K.

König, E. *Das Deuteronomium.* (Leipzig, 1917).

———. *Die Genesis*². (Gütersloh, 1925).

———. *Die Psalmen.* (Gütersloh, 1926).

Kraetzschmar, R. *Die Bundesvorstellung im Alten Testament.* (Marburg, 1896).

Landau, E. *Die gegensinnigen Wörter im Alt- u. Neuhebräischen.* (Berlin, 1896).

Lane, E. W. *An Arabic-English Lexicon.* (London, 1865).

Luther, Martin. *Die Deutsche Bibel.* Vol. II, in "Luthers Werke." (Weimar, 1909).

Marti, K. *Das Dodekapropheton.* (Tübingen, 1904). H.C.

———. *Das Buch Jesaia.* (Tübingen, 1900). H.C.

Merx, A. *Das Gedicht von Hiob.* (Jena, 1871).

Nöldeke, T. *Neue Beiträge zur Semitischen Sprachwissenschaft.* (Strassburg, 1910).
Nowack, W. *Die Kleinen Propheten.* (Göttingen, 1922). H.K.
———. *Lehrbuch der Hebräischen Archäologie.* (Freiburg i. B. und Leipzig, 1894).
———. *Richter, Ruth und Bücher Samuelis.* (Göttingen, 1902). H.K.
Orelli, C. v. *Die zwölf kleinen Propheten.* (München, 1908). K.K.
———. *Der Prophet Jeremia.* (München, 1905). K.K.
———. *Der Prophet Jesaia.* (München, 1904). K.K.
Pedersen, J. *Der Eid bei den Semiten.* (Strassburg, 1914).
Perles, F. *Analekten zur Textkritik des Alten Testaments.* New series. (Leipzig, 1922).
Procksch, O. *Die Genesis*[2,3]. (Leipzig, 1924). K.
———. *Die kleinen Prophetischen Schriften vor dem Exil.* (Stuttgart, 1910).
Reuss, E. *Das Alte Testament.* Vol. I. (Braunschweig, 1892).
Ryssel, V. *Die Synonyma des Wahren und Guten in den Semit. Sprachen.* (Leipzig, 1872).
Schmidt, H. *Die grossen Propheten*[2]. (Göttingen, 1923). A.S.
Schulthess, F. *Homonyme Wurzeln im Syrischen.* (Berlin, 1900).
Sellin, E. *Einleitung in das Alte Testament.* (Leipzig, 1925).
———. *Das Zwölfprophetenbuch.* (Leipzig, Erlangen, 1922).
Smith, H. P. *A Critical and Exegetical Commentary on the Books of Samuel.* (Edinburgh, 1904). I.C.C.
Smith, W. R. *Kinship and Marriage in Early Arabia.* (Cambridge, 1885).
———. *The Prophets of Israel.* (Edinburgh, 1882).
Stade, B. *Geschichte des Volkes Israel.* (Berlin, 1887).
Staerk, W. *Die Entstehung des Alten Testaments.* (Berlin and Leipzig, 1918).
———. *Die Lyrik*[2]. (Göttingen, 1920). A.S.
Steuernagel, C. *Deuteronomium und Josua*[2]. (Göttingen, 1923). H.K.
———. *Lehrbuch der Einleitung in das Alte Testament.* (Tübingen, 1912).
Strack, H. *Die Sprüche Salomos.* (Nördlingen, 1888). K.K.
Volz, P. *Der Prophet Jeremia.* (Leipzig, 1922). K.
———. *Weisheit.* (Göttingen, 1921). A.S.
Wellhausen, J. *Die kleinen Propheten.* (Berlin, 1898).
———. *Der Text der Bücher Samuelis.* (Göttingen, 1871).
Wildeboer, G. *Die Sprüche.* (Freiburg i. B., 1897). H.C.

Appendix

COMPARISON BETWEEN *ḤESED* AND حشد.

In the first chapter it was established that *ḥesed* is conduct based upon a mutual relationship of rights and duties. For example, the members of a clan or of an alliance were obligated to aid one another. The relative or allied individual, or to whomever else one owed an obligation, had to be protected at the price of one's possessions and even one's life. In *ḥesed* we recognized the kind of conduct entailing this mutual readiness to help.

In the second chapter we saw that *ḥesed* is the conduct corresponding to a reciprocal relationship of all men. *Ḥesed* represents the religious and ethical obligation of all men to practice humaneness and to render assistance. Although in that chapter *ḥesed* could have been translated generally as "religiosity," the basic significance of the concept of mutual aid is retained even in this broadened meaning.

In Chapter III it was shown that God's *ḥesed* is His conduct stemming from the covenant between Him and His faithful, in accordance with which He renders them assistance.

It is in Arabic that we find a striking confirmation of this fundamental characteristic of *ḥesed* — the readiness of covenanted parties for mutual aid and assistance. Among others, Schulthess points to this connection between חסד and حشد. He says: "If we accept the writing of ס as a persistent cacography with ש, we could well compare the word with the Arabic حشد, 'to band together in order to render someone assistance.' "[1] Brugsch[2] translates حشد with "assembling

[1] Schulthess, *Homonyme Wurzeln im Syrischen* (Berlin, 1900), p. 32; cf. Landau, *Die gegensinnigen Wörter im Alt- und Neuhebräischen* (Berlin, 1896), p. 45; Smith, *Prophets*, p. 406, note 9; however, against this, Nöldeke, *Neue Beiträge zur Semitischen Sprachwissenschaft* (Strassburg, 1910), p. 93.

Nöldeke compares the Aramaic *ḥesed* ܚܣܕ with the Hebrew חסד. He says: "It is more likely that we have here the development of two different meanings out of one root; there are various possibilities as to how the transitions came about, but nothing can be stated with certainty." Cf. Haupt, AJSL, Vol. 26, p. 241. Against this, Schulthess, *loc. cit.*: "The Aramaic *ḥesed* ܚܣܕ seems also to have a different

in a hurry in order to rush to someone's aid." Lane[3] translates حشد: "They collected themselves together and came round about aiding one another"; حشدوا عليه, "they collected themselves together, aiding one another against him"; احتشد as "he exerted himself for the entertainment of guests." We have shown in the first chapter that *ḥesed* is the expected mode of behavior between host and guest.[4] Brugsch translates various forms of حشد by "to assemble for mutual aid," "to make common cause against an enemy." احتشد, he renders with "to be ready (to help)"; حَشْدٌ "ready to help"; حشودة, "assistance."

The concept of mutual aid which proved to be the basic meaning of the biblical expression is then characteristic also of the Arabic word.

---

root from the Hebrew word. Of the same opinion are Landau, *loc. cit.*, Smith, *loc. cit.*

Ḥesed as "shame," "disgrace" (cf. Lev. 20:17; Prov. 14:34; 25:10) would then be the opposite of *ḥesed* in the meaning determined. Under this would be understood behavior which offends against the mutual relationship of rights and duties within the community. Such an action would be the forbidden sexual intercourse between brother and sister, which in Lev. 20:17 is branded חסד. Such an action was punished by expulsion from the community and death. Dr. H. Torczyner called my attention to the possibility of this meaning.

Ryssel, *Die Synonyma des Wahren und Guten in den Semitischen Sprachen* (Leipzig, 1872), p. 49, derives חסד from حسن *stringere*. That derivation is not very convincing.

[2] Brugsch, *Arabisch-Deutsches Handwörterbuch* (Hannover, 1924) f.

[3] Lane, *An Arabic-English Lexicon* (London, 1865).

[4] Smith, *loc. cit.*, compares חסד with the Arabic root "HSHD, in which the idea of friendly combination appears to lie, in correspondence with the fact that in Hebrew חסד is the virtue that knits together society. It is noteworthy that *ḥashada* has a special application, in the phrase *ḥashadû lahu*, to the joint exercise of hospitality to a guest."

Printed in the USA
CPSIA information can be obtained
at www.ICGtesting.com
CBHW031733130124
3410CB00003B/5

9 781610 971249